I Am
Wings Of
Freedom

DEBBIE RYE

A spiritual journey of awakening leading me
to fulfil my Divine life purpose

BALBOA.
PRESS
A DIVISION OF HAY HOUSE

Balboa Press books may be ordered through booksellers or by contacting:

Balboa Press
A Division of Hay House
1663 Liberty Drive
Bloomington, IN 47403
www.balboapress.com
1 (877) 407-4847

Because of the dynamic nature of the Internet, any web addresses or links contained in this book may have changed since publication and may no longer be valid. The views expressed in this work are solely those of the author and do not necessarily reflect the views of the publisher, and the publisher hereby disclaims any responsibility for them.

The author of this book does not dispense medical advice or prescribe the use of any technique as a form of treatment for physical, emotional, or medical problems without the advice of a physician, either directly or indirectly. The intent of the author is only to offer information of a general nature to help you in your quest for emotional and spiritual well-being. In the event you use any of the information in this book for yourself, which is your constitutional right, the author and the publisher assume no responsibility for your actions.

Any people depicted in stock imagery provided by Thinkstock are models, and such images are being used for illustrative purposes only.
Certain stock imagery © Thinkstock.

Printed in the United States of America.

ISBN: 978-1-4525-2307-1 (sc)
ISBN: 978-1-4525-2309-5 (hc)
ISBN: 978-1-4525-2308-8 (e)

Library of Congress Control Number: 2014917966

Balboa Press rev. date: 11/07/2014

My Guardian Angel – 'Excelsior'

Channelled Artwork by Jayne Franz.

This book is dedicated to my husband Len,
my children Christian and Jason
and to my dad, Nick Gurney, now in spirit.

CONTENTS

FOREWORD

I have been calling upon the skills of Debbie Rye to clear negative energies for several years now. Wherever I am in the world I meet people who are living in "haunted" houses, sick buildings and in some cases their lives have become a struggle because of the presence of difficult and dark spirits in their homes. Without fail Debbie has pinpointed the problem, not always what it would seem, and cleared the troublesome energies. Imagine the relief for people who shed bad health, insomnia and other physical problems all caused by energies, entities and souls that they cannot see but that have destroyed their peace and wellbeing for years. Debbie has helped people all over the world and she does this without even stepping on a plane!

So I was delighted to receive her book to review – what an opportunity to read the story behind these magical transformations to places and people and to find out how she discovered the amazing gifts she uses. When I started the book I was aware of her magical pendulum but I had no idea what a journey she has followed to get her to the confident and accomplished dowser and healer that she is today.

As you read you will see how her own health issues have led her to the path of discovery. As she opened to alternative ways of healing she healed her candida. She then went on to discover the cause of her insomnia and low energy levels. This path led her to the understanding that the energy in houses can hold negative imprints, be affected by earth energies, spirit interference and the effects of past conflicts. As more and more became clear and she discovered she could clear these troublesome energies for herself she was drawn to help others with their own "sick houses". She is now one of the country's leading dowsers and energy clearers.

Through sharing her own story Debbie helps us to understand some of the mysteries of life and in a simple and down to earth way she opens the door to the unseen world around you. I am confident that this book will help you to open your mind and perception to the bigger picture of the world in which you live and through this understanding I am sure you will be inspired and empowered as Debbie shows how you can take control of your environment and not be the victim of it.

Debbie's work is all about turning a negative situation into a positive one from her desire to heal herself that rewarded her with her gift to the way she uses that gift to transform energies for other people. This is the ripple effect which is the way we can ourselves make a difference; as we smile, help strangers, see the positive in situations we are shining light onto the darkness that brings suffering and confusion. Remember that, without a doubt, the light is more powerful than the dark – just enter a dark room and switch on the light to see which wins. Debbie's work demonstrates this over and over again.

Anne Jones
Spiritual healer, author and seminar speaker.
www.annejones.org
www.the-powerofyou.co.uk

ACKNOWLEDGEMENTS

Firstly I must thank my husband Len, and two sons, Christian and Jason, for supporting me on my spiritual journey and putting up with me during some very weird times.

I am grateful to my sister Jayne for the wonderful painting of my guardian angel, Excelsior, that she channelled for the back cover of this book and the joyous angelic energy can now be carried wherever the book goes.

Special thanks to my editor, Dr. Geoffrey Williams, for his editing skills and valuable advice.

I want to thank my dear friend, Caroline Izzard, for her insights and readings during the early years of my journey.

I would especially like to thank Marlene Williams who was my Earth angel, always at the end of the telephone and ready to do clearing and SRT on me when I went through a difficult period.

On a personal level, I would like to thank two friends, Nicki Nunn and Jo Duffy. Nicki's monthly crystal and reflexology sessions have helped to keep my physical and energy bodies in good shape. Before moving to Scotland, Jo's Evolved Soul Healing Sessions were a highlight of the month for me. They were tremendously helpful and supportive to my spiritual growth.

I must thank Anne Jones for proof reading the first draft of this book and giving me encouragement to go forwards with it.

Thanks also to Suzanne Stiles and Pamilla Cobb for proof reading the manuscript. Thank you Pam for your sound advice on how to go about getting my book published.

I offer my gratitude to Unity and Daily Word for their kind permission to include some of their affirmations in this book.

Another thank you to my dear husband Len for his computer and technology skills without which I would be lost.

A thank you list wouldn't be complete without mentioning my wonderful clients for bringing me the opportunities to work with the angels, trying new techniques and providing such useful feedback.

Last, but by no means least, huge gratitude to my angels, Archangels, Ascended Masters, my Higher Self and God for being ever present and guiding me on my path.

INTRODUCTION

In April 2000 we moved to a cottage within our village where I saw that an Angel Workshop was to be held across the road from my new home. I decided to go as I felt it would help me find the answers to some of the problems I had been experiencing for several months. The workshop opened my eyes to the world of angels and a whole new sphere of information which had been previously unknown to me. It was the start of my journey to where I am today, working as an energy healer and, in particular, healing the earth. The angels stepped in to be my teachers and guides, literally arriving on my doorstep when the time was right. During the following four years the angels taught me through personal experience how to clear earthbound souls and dark entities of every type from people and buildings. They showed me how to restore balance and harmony in peoples' lives by healing the various detrimental energies found in the earth beneath their houses. The lessons were constant and often painful until the angels had taught me all I needed to know for my earth healing work.

Many clients were keen to learn more about my work and I started to hold small workshops at home. After describing some of my experiences people were always interested to hear more and many told me that I should write a book. As these requests continued, I took it as a sign from the angels that I should put pen to paper. Writing didn't come easily to me so I put it off for quite a while and especially as I was so busy. I attended Evolved Soul healing sessions which my friend Jo Duffy held monthly at her home nearby. There were three regulars, my friends

Nicki and Lauren and myself. We would sit in meditation, holding the Light, whilst Jo took it in turns to work with each of us. In November 2011 I was at one of Jo's sessions and was in meditation and not listening to what she was telling Nicki, when suddenly her words "universal library" seemed to burst into my conscious mind. I immediately saw a huge library and recognised my book which appeared to be floating towards me, an angel on either side of it. "Oh that's my book", I remarked to the angels. The angels said, "This is your book, but you have to write it". I told them I was too busy at present and would have to wait until my business slowed down. They told me the business would not slow down but only increase and I had to fit the writing of the book around my work. This was quite a commanding instruction from the angels and so two days later I sat down at my computer and made a start. Even though it has taken me over two years of struggle to complete, it has given me quite a sense of achievement now that it has been done. I hope you will enjoy reading my story.

CHAPTER

Our Dream Home

I sat in my little meditation room at home, my charts on my lap, pendulum in hand and connected with my Higher Self. I was dowsing a property for a new client in Cornwall who had been experiencing many problems since living in their house which had the old Roman road Foss Way running alongside it. I had dowsed that the property had geopsychic stress, which means it had psychic presences of earthbound souls, or entities, or what some would call ghosts. I started my clearing process to send these presences on to the Light, my pendulum swinging quickly indicating that clearing was taking place. My pendulum swung round and round rapidly and in my mind's eye I could see an endless stream of souls passing over to the Light. They looked like Roman soldiers marching up to Heaven. When eventually my pendulum became still, I made sure there were no more and then closed the openings over the building. I asked how many souls had been rescued and found it was in excess of 3,000. They had been stuck in Earth's energies for a long time but now within a few minutes had been returned safely to the Light.

There was also a negative energetic pattern on the land which is usually the result of a battle or similar, so I healed this to bring the land back into balance again.

You may wonder how I have got involved with doing such unusual work. Well, if anyone had told me fifteen years ago that I would be doing this sort of work in houses all over the world, I would have thought them crazy. I knew nothing about any such subjects. I didn't have any psychic powers and didn't really know much about intuition or signs from the Universe. Apart from having a few premonitions at different times in my life and the occasional déjà vu experiences, I was an 'ordinary' housewife and mother living with my husband Len and two sons Christian and Jason. I had always believed in life after death and was quite fascinated when I came across articles about psychics, mediums and healers and thought how wonderful that they had been 'chosen' for those gifts.

My spiritual journey really began when Len decided he wanted to build a house himself and we set out trying to buy a building plot. We wanted to stay in the village where we lived in Cambridgeshire and tried for a number of sites, but always lost out to builders. A good sized plot then came on the market just round the corner from where we lived. It was for sale by sealed bid and belonged to a local farmer. The site had been his slaughter house, although hadn't been used since the 1940s.

Knowing nothing of spirits or energies, this didn't worry us. It was just an overgrown plot of land but perfect for us to build our dream home. I had a very strong premonition that we would live there. A few days later a gypsy called at my house selling lace and table cloths. As she showed me her basket of goods she started telling me various things about me and my family. She was very accurate and I was interested to hear more, so I looked more seriously at the table cloths. She told me that we would be getting a new car within a week. This seemed strange as we had no intention of changing our car. Then she said we would be moving soon to another house. Immediately I got a mental image identical to my premonition and felt quite excited. I thanked her, bought a table cloth and started wondering how accurate she would prove to be.

I told Len about the gypsy, but he was sceptical about such things saying it was all nonsense and guess work. Three or four days later Len's mother called to say her widowed friend had decided to sell her late husband's beloved Ford Orion. It was in excellent condition, had extremely low mileage and was at a very good price. The offer seemed too good to miss, but it would leave us with a high mileage Ford Cortina to sell. The next evening as Len was coming home, our neighbour told him that their very old car had completely packed up and they would have to try and find something soon. When he said we might be getting a new car ourselves and would she be interested in ours, she was over the moon. So, just like the gypsy said, within a week we had a new car!

I felt this also meant she was right about our getting a new home and felt very confident that we would be successful in buying the slaughter house site. I was so confident that I didn't worry about the fact we had to put in a sealed bid. The market price for a building plot of this size back in the mid 80s was about £35,000, so we added on a bit and sent in our bid. I could envisage us living there in our new house and had no doubts that it would happen. I was so confident that we almost bought a second hand mobile home in which to live on site whilst we were building. Thankfully, something stopped us from buying the mobile home for if we didn't get the land we would have had nowhere to keep it.

When the day came to find out if we had been successful, we were gutted to find out we hadn't won the bid. A builder had got it instead. I couldn't believe it. It had just felt so right.

The good thing, however, was that I was a few months pregnant and I had been dreading the thought of my second child being born in a mobile home. When Christian was born we painted his nursery and furnished it, Len made a wooden crib and I made some lovely crib bedding in Broderie Anglais. There were mobiles and pictures hanging up and cuddly toys arranged around the room. It was perfect for a baby's room.

I had suffered two miscarriages before becoming pregnant with Jason. I was trying to take things easy, anxious in case I miscarried a third time, and with hindsight the stress of living in a mobile home and building a house would have made things worse. Coupled with the thought that my second baby would be denied the lovely nursery that had been Christian's, there was definitely a blessing in losing the land.

So I concentrated on looking after myself and we decided to delay looking for any more building plots until after the baby was born. I often walked past the old slaughter house to see what was happening, but nothing ever was. Eventually the 'SOLD' sign was taken down and it remained the overgrown site I had always known it to be since moving to the village.

Apart from developing pregnancy related diabetes at 28 weeks, the pregnancy went well and I gave birth to my wonderful baby, Jason, late in 1987. I was so pleased that he started life in a lovely house with his pretty nursery and surrounded by all the soft toys and musical mobiles that Christian had so enjoyed.

Once Jason was a few months old we both began wondering what was going to happen to the old slaughter house site. Len made some enquiries with the agents and farmer and discovered that the owner had lost the deeds so the sale was delayed by a legal process which would enable him to sell it. The buyer had pulled out and it was likely to be another twelve months or so before it could be sold. That enabled us to buy the plot at the market price without competition from builders.

We finally completed the purchase just prior to Jason's second birthday. We also decided to rent a small cottage while our house was being built rather than live on site in a mobile home. It felt a daunting step to move out of our lovely home into a small terraced cottage while only owning an overgrown plot of land, but once planning permission was sorted, demolition was out of the way and the foundations were finished, we became very excited about our project.

The building work went very smoothly. Knowing what I do now about blocked earth energies this is quite surprising, but we felt that higher powers ensured all went well. There were hardly any frosts that winter and the spring was warm and dry so building work was never delayed. Len started his working life as a telephone engineer and then progressed to computer programming, but had always been very keen on DIY. He had done an evening class in brick laying and built an extension on our last house and now realised his ambition of building his own home. It was a timber framed kit house so that speeded up the whole process, but apart from having the timber frame erected professionally and employing plasterers to render the outside, he did everything himself - along with help from me, our parents and two very eager little boys! We moved into the almost completed house about eleven months later.

"Everything is in Perfect and Divine Order Right Now"

CHAPTER

Candida

We had chosen all the fixtures and fittings and were delighted with what had became our dream home. We lived happily enjoying family life. I felt very contented and didn't feel I was stressed in any way, but after about five years the diabetes I had suffered from in pregnancy returned. Initially I treated it by adjusting my diet, then my doctor prescribed tablets but I had a terrible reaction and was put onto insulin. This made it much easier to keep my blood sugar levels down but it meant I had to eat far more carbohydrates and so my consumption of bread increased at this time.

Over the following year I started to suffer from bloating, stomach ache and headaches. It built up gradually until it became a constant problem. I had always believed that health was about diet and exercise. I loved walking and keeping fit and had always eaten a healthy diet although I admit to having a sweet tooth as well. I could not understand why I was feeling so bloated and uncomfortable. By the latter part of each day I couldn't do up my jeans and although I was young and slim I had to start looking for clothes with expanding waistbands.

I read about someone with similar symptoms in a health magazine and it was suggested they had a digestive intolerance to wheat. I decided to try cutting wheat out of my diet and I felt much better within a day or two. However, after about three weeks the symptoms started to return. I then decided to cut the other gluten containing grains out of my diet and this helped again. I felt more comfortable, but my diet was becoming restricted. The feeling of improvement didn't last long so I cut dairy products from my diet. Again I experienced some improvement, but it didn't last so I made an appointment to see the doctor. He diagnosed Irritable Bowel Syndrome (IBS) and prescribed some gluten free foods. Other than that he could only say it was related to stress.

I read up about IBS and couldn't understand why I should have it. My health then deteriorated rapidly over the following year and I developed aches and pains in all my joints, I became lethargic and depressed. I had no energy and I wasn't sleeping properly. Every morning I woke with a head ache, or fuzzy head. My back ached all the way up my spine so that I couldn't sit in an armchair and had to sit in a firm dining chair. I was 39 years old but felt like 90.

I was becoming a regular visitor to the doctor's surgery although they didn't seem able to help and eventually I was referred to the gastroenterology department of the hospital. I began a series of tests but none of them showed the problem and all the time I was getting worse.

My only experience of alternative or complementary therapies had been several years previously when I decided to do an evening class to get me out of the house and do something that didn't involve the children. I had scanned the adult education classes at the local school and noticed a class on Reflexology. This appealed straight away as I had always loved having my feet massaged and it intrigued me that this could have health benefits.

I duly enrolled and enjoyed learning about reflexology for the next six months. The teacher, June, was also trained in aromatherapy massage and herbs so I followed the reflexology with these classes as well. I found them very interesting but at the time I was perfectly healthy so I didn't follow it up. I did keep June's business card, however, just in case I should need her help in the future.

Now, several years later I was undergoing tests at hospital and June's card fell out of my handbag. I hadn't seen it for some years and didn't even know I still had it. I wondered if she could help me with all my problems but told myself that reflexology and massage wouldn't be any good and put it back again. The card fell out again a few months later and I went through the same mental conversation with myself, but again decided it would be a waste of time to get in touch. I struggled on for several more weeks and the hospital then suggested one more test. As I was getting ready to go for my appointment, my handbag fell over on the bed and the card slipped out again. I know now of course that the Universe or my angels and guides were trying to give me a message, but I was still unaware then of how things worked. I decided that if this test was negative, I would contact June and arrange for some massage to try and ease my aches and pains.

After spending about five hours at the hospital the nurse told me that nothing was showing up and so the doctor was going to put me onto the 'total exclusion' diet in the new year. The doctor explained that this would involve me eating only chicken and pears for two weeks, returning to hospital to see if I had any symptoms and then adding in rice as well for the next two weeks. He said I would continue like this for maybe a year or even two until they could work out exactly what I could eat. The thought of this filled me with horror. There was no way the total exclusion diet would get me better, so I decided to take my life and health back into my own hands.

I telephoned June and made an appointment for some treatment a couple of days later. The experience was so different from hospital. I spent two hours having reflexology and massage and she listened to all my problems. June felt sure I had an overgrowth of candida bacteria in the gut and recommended her programme of herbs and vitamins to clear it. I had never heard of candida before and wondered why the doctors had never mentioned it.

Candida albicans is a yeast based bacteria found in everyone's gut. Ideally it should be in a ratio of no more than 20% candida to 80% healthy gut flora and at this level it causes no problems. Various factors can cause it to grow excessively and then it can become a major problem. As it proliferates it changes form and can burrow through the gut walls creating little holes which let particles of food escape into the body. The body reacts to the escaped particles of food so you develop a digestive intolerance. The candida bacteria can also migrate to other areas of the body and lodge into joints, organs and even the brain.

The symptoms can be many and varied and cause joint aches and pain, headaches, blocked sinuses, skin problems, chemical intolerances as well the obvious dietary problems.

I arranged to have a Vega test done a few days later and this confirmed all the foods I had a problem with and the practitioner confirmed an overgrowth of candida. Two complimentary therapists had come up with the same cause.

There was no doubt in my mind that I had to give this a try and so I started on the herbal programme to cleanse and detoxify the body and then re-populate the gut with healthy gut flora, taking anti-fungal herbs, with lots of vitamins and minerals to help strengthen my immune system. My diet was so restricted as I was already following an anti-candida diet, but now had to cut out all fresh fruit as well.

Within four or five weeks I started to notice a big difference. The uncomfortable bloating had finally gone and I was able to re-introduce fresh fruits and some dairy. The aches and pains in my joints had started to lessen and I was feeling much more positive. I was so impressed that I wanted to learn more about the herbs and supplements and start selling them to help other people. Despite feeling so unwell for so long I had also been feeling that I should be doing something else with my life because I didn't want to return to office work and this really appealed.

I think because I made the decision to go in that direction, which was what my soul wanted me to do, I got better very quickly. I learnt about the herbs and Len made me a web site to start selling them.

"I Let Go and Let God"

CHAPTER

Awakening

Although my digestive problems continued to improve, I still suffered from poor sleep and daily headaches. These were often so bad that they woke me at about three or four each morning. I would come downstairs and take painkillers and then sit in the armchair with a pillow and blanket. I couldn't bear to go back to bed. I would sit for a couple of hours until the headache eased and then doze until the children got up for breakfast, but it would take till mid morning before I felt my energy levels start to lift.

I hated taking painkillers on a daily basis and was determined to find the cause of these debilitating headaches, so I worked my way through all the natural remedies to solve the problem. I tried each supplement for at least three or four months, but nothing made any difference.

This pattern continued for about eighteen months with the headaches getting worse rather than better. We booked a fortnight's holiday in an old granary in East Sussex. I was worried that my headaches and lack of energy would spoil things for the boys and I always tried to keep from them how rough I felt. I packed a supply of pain killers to last the holiday plus a selection of supplements.

We arrived at our lovely holiday home with its big garden, swimming pool and tennis court and made ourselves at home. We went to bed that night tired from the journey and exploring the property and I fell asleep in no time. The next thing I knew it was morning and my first thought on waking was "I don't have a headache". What an amazing feeling that was. I checked my watch and it was past seven am. I felt so refreshed and good and believed at last that my combination of supplements was right and something had finally kicked in. The energy of the environment never entered my head as it was then something I knew nothing about.

As the fortnight passed I continued to sleep like a baby with more energy each day. I was outside playing tennis with the boys by eight am and just felt amazing. I didn't get a single headache for the whole holiday and the painkillers came home unopened. I felt sure I was on my way to good health again.

Having returned home feeling so energised and refreshed, I wasn't expecting the terrible night's sleep and headache on my first night back in my own bed. I talked to Len about what it could be and we decided it had to be our bed. We knew that in the holiday home the bed was brand new so the next weekend we spent quite a lot of money on a lovely new bed.

It felt so comfortable when we got into bed that night, but it made no difference. I dare not get up in the early hours with my thumping head as Len had just parted with a lot of money which we had thought would solve the problem. I told him in the morning it would take me a few days for my spine to adjust to the bed but of course, this made no difference and the pattern continued.

I tried special pillows to support the neck and spine, but the headaches went on. About six months later we were going away with the rest of the family to Centre Parcs for an Easter break. There were thirteen of us and the boys were so excited to be going away with their cousins. We had been to Centre Parcs several times and it was always a busy time, swimming, cycling and playing badminton. I was wondering how on earth I would keep up with everyone else with my lethargy and headaches each day and again I packed a supply of painkillers for the stay.

It was as if a switch had been flicked inside me, I slept so well, felt full of energy and my headaches disappeared. We had a lovely energetic break and on the last morning before leaving I sat with my mum, sister and sister-in-law having coffee in one of the cafés and my sister in law remarked how energetic Len had been. I told her he was always like that on holidays and then thought about what I had said. Len didn't suffer from the terrible headaches but he certainly always had more energy when away from home. I began to wonder if there was something in the house that was poisoning us. I decided that if my sleep pattern returned when we got home, I would have to investigate that possibility.

By pure chance my mother also asked me if I knew anything about magnetic therapy for treating arthritis. I had heard about it and said I would find out more. I felt certain that June would know something about it.

Once again we returned from a lovely holiday for me to have the same sleep and headache pattern return, although I knew in my heart that this would be the case. I said a prayer; asking for help to discover what it was. I knew there was something and I presumed it was a chemical used in the building materials. I had no idea how to go about finding out as this was before the internet was so comprehensive.

I also rang June to enquire about magnetic healing and she gave me the name of a magnetic healing machine and the 'phone number of the company that sold it. I rang on behalf of my mother to ask for the price of this machine and the company took my details and said they would send some information. A few days later a large pack arrived with all sorts of information leaflets. There was one leaflet entitled Geopathic Stress. I put it to one side as this meant nothing to me and looked through for the price of the magnetic healing machine. It was quite expensive and beyond my mum's budget, so it was forgotten. About four days later I sat down for a cup of tea with a spare hour as Jason was going to a friend's house from school. I decided to read the leaflet on Geopathic Stress. I read the first few sentences and knew immediately that I had found the answer. I couldn't believe what I was reading and wondered why I had never heard about it before, but I felt excited with this new information.

"I Am a Great and Powerful Master of the Light"

CHAPTER

Dowsing

As soon as I had read the leaflet I telephoned the dowser who had written it and managed to speak to him immediately. He dowsed me over the 'phone and confirmed that I did have one line or ray of Geopathic Stress running through my house and he said this line went through my bed. He dowsed that 95% of my headaches were caused by this and suggested I buy his neutraliser. I got the credit card out straight away even though it was quite costly, but I just had to give this a try.

The neutraliser arrived a day or two later. It consisted of a tall metal box that plugged into the electricity socket. Len wasn't very impressed with it and didn't hold out any hope that it would work. Amazingly, the following morning I woke up free from a headache and I had slept all night. Len felt sure this was psychological, but I knew differently. After six consecutive nights with deep sleep and no pain I felt relieved and also very curious to know more about the subject. I rang the dowser to give him some feedback, asked a number of questions and purchased his book.

I couldn't put the book down. I was amazed at the information which I knew in my heart was true. I found out that Geopathic Stress (GS) is a term for underground faults and stream lines in the Earth, maybe hundreds of feet below the surface. These lines of vibrations were measured in cycles, Hertz per second, and affect the body particularly where we are lying for the long hours of sleep. The normal level of Hertz vibrations is measured at 7.8 Hertz per second but when you have got GS, the frequency of the Hertz vibrations can become as high as 300 cycles per second or higher. The effect of a high level of Hz vibrations in the brain is to prevent deep restful sleep. The human body is designed to carry out many self healing abilities whilst we sleep, such as repairing cells, fighting infections, assimilating nutrients and so forth. Obviously if you do not get to the deep level of sleep your body cannot carry out such functions and so over time your immune system is lowered. This made perfect sense with what had happened to me.

I made a set of dowsing rods using metal coat hangers and biro casings and then went into the garden to try and find the ray of GS. Len and the boys were watching me with amusement as I walked slowly across the garden asking to be shown any GS. Suddenly the rods opened out and stayed in this position for a while then closed back again. This matched the position of the ray of GS that the dowser had found. I was greeted with shouts of "you did that", "you were moving them", but I assured the boys that I wasn't. Len then demanded to have a go himself and the rods did the same thing. He looked shocked and put them down quickly. I don't think he has tried dowsing again to this day. The boys also tried and the results were the same.

I felt a strong urge to tell other people about my new found knowledge. I had now been sleeping well and free of headaches for about six weeks and I was keen to help other people. I started telling friends and family, neighbours and other mums at school, especially those that had suffered ill health. I expected people to be interested and grateful about what I had discovered, but soon realised that nobody believed me or wanted to know. Most people thought I had lost the plot and backed away from me. Others suggested it was just psychological but if it helped me then that was fine.

One of my friends, Jane, was interested though. It turned out she had heard about GS several years beforehand and she was eager for me to come over to her house and try out my new found skill with the dowsing rods.

Jane's house was one of a group of about seven or eight that had been built in the early 1970s on some disused farm land. Jane and her family had suffered all sorts of problems and health issues since living there and had also experienced psychic phenomena. I didn't know at the time but she had had mediums and healers of all types out to the house to try and sort out the problems. Jane and her husband had researched the history of the land and found that it was most likely the site of a terrible accident that happened in the village in 1727.

The tragic accident that happened on 8th September 1727 is well known in the village. A travelling puppeteer stopped at the village and performed a puppet show in a barn. Many of the villagers came to the show, including families from neighbouring villages. It was a very windy evening and had been an extremely dry summer. The barn was very large and had a partition with stacked hay bales filling one side. The barn soon filled up with the people paying the one penny entrance. There was a very narrow doorway into the barn and an oval table was placed in front of the door to stop it blowing open in the wind. A stable lad turned up at the barn after the show had started and tried to gain entrance free of charge as he had no money. Entrance was refused and so he managed to get into the side of the barn and climb up high on the hay stack to view from the rafters. He had a candle or lantern with him and it is thought this got knocked over and set the hay on fire. The fire quickly spread through the thatch and the barn was burnt down.

There were 140 people at the puppet show and 78 perished. People died from every single family in the village. Some families lost all their children. Bodies were so badly burned that in the following days local people searched the embers and collected limbs and body parts and these were all put together in two pits. There is still a flaming heart commemorative grave stone in the village churchyard. This land then remained vacant for the following 250 years or so until sold by the council for houses.

One of the mediums that came to Jane's house had seen many spirit children in the house and also a man wearing a black cloak and a black tri corn hat. She had tried to get the spirits to go but without success.

Another healer came out to try and suggested placing saucers of milk at the doorways and sprinkling salt all around the house. This also had no effect on the goings on in the house.

So I arrived at Jane's with my dowsing rods still unaware of what she had found out. I walked around the house and garden and was amazed by all the lines I was finding. My house had been quite simple in comparison with just one line but here they were criss-crossing all over the place. Also as I walked with my rods I started to feel very ill. I didn't understand at the time but by using the rods and asking to find GS, I was drawing the GS up into my body. My head was thumping and I was shaking. I couldn't wait to leave. I had only been there about an hour but I felt so ill that I went home to bed where it took about two or three hours for the energy to drain out of my body again.

The next week a mutual friend of mine and Jane contacted me and asked if I would dowse her house as well. She lived in a neighbouring village and by now I had fully recovered from the previous experience and was keen to give the dowsing another go. I spent about an hour walking about with my rods and also found that her house had several lines of GS. The effects on my body were even worse than at Jane's. I felt so ill and managed to get back home just in time before I threw up. I was shaking and my head thumping and it took a full day for me to recover.

I started to realise that I was so sensitive to these energies that there was no way I could put my body through it again and so I couldn't possibly dowse anyone else's house. However, I also felt deeply within that I had found out about this for a reason and I was supposed to inform people about these negative energies and how badly they could affect your life.

I was selling herbs and vitamin supplements to people, but I knew that if they were living in GS then they wouldn't be able to recover until this was cleared. I had been taking supplements to treat my candida for a long time and it wasn't until the GS was cleared that I could gradually reduce and stop them so I felt it was important I let my clients know or they could be spending so much money on supplements without end.

I referred back to the dowsing book and re-read the section again on distant dowsing. The author stated that if you can dowse with rods you can distant dowse with a pendulum. So I set about making a pendulum using a metal nut and a length of wool. I tried this out and it was like magic when it responded to me immediately. I made a chart as shown in the book and started dowsing. It seemed to come naturally to me. I dowsed my supplements and the food in the fridge and asked lots of questions. It was great fun! Although it's not ethical I dowsed a number of my family from my address book and found that those who had suffered health problems were in some degree of GS whereas those that seemed to sail through life free from ailments were living in good energies. I felt confident in this new found skill and realised that this was how I could dowse houses for people.

It was about two months now since I had purchased my neutraliser and I was feeling so well, getting deep sleep and no more awful headaches and then suddenly the headaches and disturbed sleep returned. What I didn't realise at that time was that by dowsing with a pendulum I had opened myself up psychically very quickly and was now becoming sensitive to other energies. I couldn't bear to go back to the previous pattern again so contacted the dowser. He re-dowsed the house and said I needed to upgrade to a stronger machine which I did. This made no difference. I upgraded again and eventually had the industrial model neutraliser but still this made no difference. The dowser was unable to offer any other help.

It was awful going back to sleepless nights and terrible headaches. I felt I really couldn't continue to live in our lovely house and so Len reluctantly agreed that we should put the house on the market. We had so many viewings and everyone seemed to fall in love with the house but then something would always happen to make them change their minds and so no offers came.

I was starting to feel desperate and didn't know what to do so I contacted the British Society of Dowsers to find another dowser who could help me. I was put in touch with a lady. She wanted to know the history of my house and I explained it was new and we had built it ourselves. She enquired whether I knew anything about the history of the land and I responded that it had been a slaughter house. She gasped in horror and then told me that the house was full of spirits, which she called geopsychic stress. I needed further clarification on this as it was a totally new subject to me. She explained a bit about souls not always passing to the Light when they die and becoming stuck in earth's energies. She also talked about the fear and pain that would be held in the earth under the house because repeated killing had taken place there.

From my experiences since then, I have learned that when people die their soul or spirit is called to pass over to the Light. A gateway is opened and the Angels of Light call you to come through. Your Guardian Angel encourages you to answer the call to pass over and deceased loved ones from the spirit world may appear to encourage you over as well. However, we all have free will and so can ignore the call and choose to stay if we wish. No-one dies before their time and it is impossible for a soul to leave the earth unless they are ready to do so, but on a conscious level people are not aware of this. If someone dies suddenly and traumatically then they often don't realise they have died and this is a common cause of a soul becoming stuck in the earth's vibrations. Unfortunately it will be like a state of limbo for the soul, unable to move on and evolve. If they have died in a battle then they can be caught up in playing out their final battle scene for many years to come. Other reasons why a soul may choose to stay on Earth can be related to a personal attachment they have to money, property, a loved one, or a substance such as alcohol, tobacco or drugs. Sometimes a person may feel that they have unfinished business to attend to and this prevents them moving on at death. It seems that the gateway and the call of the angels goes on for a few days and maybe up until the funeral takes place but then it closes. If the soul still hasn't passed over then they have missed the boat and have to remain stuck until someone sends angels to collect them.

So it was a great relief to now know what this stress was and I asked the dowser if she could help. She said she would love to try although couldn't guarantee that she could clear it all. I pleaded with her to try and she then said her fee would be between £700 and £1,000. It was now my turn to gasp in horror. I wasn't earning very much at all from the herbs and Len was beginning to think I was going a bit crazy so I knew he wouldn't be prepared to pay anything like that, especially as we were selling the house. I told her this and she basically said that we wouldn't be able to sell the house and that was that.

I realise now that she was referring to the spirits in the house preventing the sale, but she didn't make that clear and was not prepared to help if we couldn't pay, despite the fact she had told me she worked for the Universe.

Strangely, some years later when I was doing soul rescue and clearances as part of my business, I was at a dowsing group meeting and I heard her name mentioned. I enquired after her and was told she had been killed in a car accident a month earlier in America. When I got home I asked whether her soul had passed to the Light, but found she was still earthbound. So I then asked if I could rescue her and send her to the Light and I got permission to do so.

"I Am Well in Body, Mind and Spirit"
Reprinted with permission from *Daily Word*® **UK**

CHAPTER

April Cottage

My understandings about the causes of illness and how to keep well were gradually being challenged and altered. From believing that health was all about diet and exercise, I had now learned from experience that sometimes the body required additional nutritional supplements and the energies of where you slept also played a big part. It seemed that being free from GS was a major factor in keeping well and now I was also discovering that geopsychic stress was also a factor to consider.

Despite having been quoted such a large figure to get the geopsychic stress cleared, I was grateful to have found out what was causing my disturbed sleep and headaches again and felt I would be able to find the right person to help.

I saw an advertisement for a Mind Body Spirit event and noticed there was a talk being given on Feng Shui and Black Streams. I had read a Feng Shui book a few years before and found the subject interesting and felt this talk may be helpful. I explained my problems to the Feng Shui consultant after her talk but she didn't seem to know anything about spirits and entities but said that sometimes you could ask the 'black streams' to go away. When I got home I dowsed if this was possible and was told yes. So I tried asking them to go away and it worked. I was finally able to get to sleep again but had to keep repeating my requests that the black streams retreat from the house.

Over the following months we kept our house on the market and despite many people saying they wanted to buy it, something always happened to change their minds. We had seen a lovely cottage for sale which I had dowsed from the picture in the paper so I knew it had good energies. It needed quite a bit of work but this gave Len plenty of projects to keep him happy and the cottage had lovely features and a lot of character. Luckily it also stayed on the market for the eight months it took to sell our home and I realise now that it was waiting for us.

Whilst managing the situation with the energies at home, I was constantly asking for help and guidance to find the right person who could help me. As I skimmed through the local paper one day an advert for a Psychic Fair jumped out at me. I immediately felt a strong intuitive feeling that there would be someone at this fair who could help and my pendulum confirmed this. I had never visited a psychic fair or been to see a psychic before and felt a bit nervous, so got another friend to come along with me.

I strolled past the stall holders looking at their signs to see if anyone mentioned that they could clear geopsychic stress. Amongst the tarot card readers, palmists and clairvoyants I could find no mention of this so I approached a friendly looking lady and asked her and she directed me to a gentleman named Pete on the stage. I told him something of my problems and he offered to come back to my house with me straight away. He wasn't worried about missing the fair as he said I was the reason he had come. First of all he had to clear my energy fields as he could see three souls attached to me. I immediately felt a lifting of pressure from my head.

He followed me back home and came into the hall way. He glanced around and said the house was full of spirits, but he felt sure he would be able to clear them all. He said it would take four or five hours and his fee was £60. This was far more reasonable and we arranged for him to come back a couple of days later. I didn't want the children to know anything about this in case they got frightened, so he agreed to come at 10:00 am and said it would be finished by the time I had to collect them from school.

The day arrived for Pete to do his work and I felt very great anticipation but also quite confident that it would work. He was late arriving as he had suffered an upset stomach, then found he was nearly out of petrol and then got a flat tyre. He said the dark forces were trying to stop him from coming to help me, but there was no way they would have succeeded.

He worked in quite a ritualistic way. We had to open all the internal doors in the house including cupboard doors and all the drawers. He lit candles and incense and played music and then lay out on the living room floor, forming a five point star. I can't imagine what the neighbours would have thought if they had seen what was going on!

Eventually the process was completed and I felt a real shift and lightening of the energies in the house. I was able to go round the house with Pete using my pendulum to check each room. He could sense something in the dining room still remaining. We had used an oak beam from the slaughter house over the inglenook fireplace and this had to be separately cleared. I then remembered we had used the old bricks from the slaughter house in the foundations so he cleared these as well.

We walked into each room and all seemed clear until we entered the internal garage. He felt a dark presence and insisted that I go back into the kitchen as it wasn't safe. I thought this sounded a little far fetched, but did as he suggested. He had to clear a very dark spirit that he said had enjoyed the killing whilst it was a slaughter house and that this spirit was the cause of some of my bad headaches.

Pete completed the process with a prayer of thanks and a blessing and then told me his guides were saying that I had to learn how to do this as this was my path. I told him there was no way I wanted anything more to do with spirits. I accepted now that they existed, but I never wanted to come into contact with one again. Little did I know what lay in store for me! I then asked him about the sale of the house and showed him a picture of the cottage we wanted to buy. He did a short meditation and said he could see a removal van outside in just a few weeks time and the cottage was very good, but a little sad in the upstairs area but my name was on the front door.

Pete left just after 3:00 pm so I quickly dashed off to school to meet the boys. They both went up to their rooms when we got in demanding to know why all their drawers and wardrobe doors were open! In my hurry I had forgotten about closing them so had to make up an excuse that I had been searching for something.

Ten days later we had an offer on the house and had our offer accepted on the cottage and the sale and purchase proceeded with ease. We moved into the lovely energies of April Cottage a few weeks later. It felt like we were on holiday for about six weeks and we both slept like babies.

During those few weeks before we moved I did have to get help from Pete on a number of occasions. About two weeks after the house had been cleared I felt something attach to me whilst I was out. I had immediate pressure on my head which turned to pain fairly quickly. I rang Pete who cleared a spirit from me distantly. He told me again that his guides were saying I had to learn to do this myself as it was my path. My response again was 'No Way'.

This happened twice more and each time Pete had to clear me. Each time he reiterated his suggestion that I would have to learn how to do this myself as it wouldn't leave me alone. However, I still resisted hoping it would just stop. Rather than stop though, it happened again very quickly. I rang Pete but he was out and so I left a message hoping he would pick it up and clear me as soon as possible.

Whilst waiting for Pete to get back to me, I put a CD in the machine to play. We had been to a concert the previous evening at Christian's school and one of his classmates had sung a solo. He had the most amazing voice and the choirmaster told us that that he had released a CD of choir music recorded in our local church. It included Ave Maria, Pie Jesu, O Holy Night amongst the selection. As I sat listening to this beautiful music, my head started to feel clearer. I was feeling very light and thought Pete had cleared me.

I then felt able to get on with things and played the CD a couple more times. Pete rang about 5:00 pm to apologise that he had been out all day and only just picked up my message. He hadn't done any clearing on me at all so when I told him what had happened he said I had cleared it myself with the help of the music.

He said I was being shown that it was much easier than I imagined and I really did need to learn to do this myself. I also hated being reliant on Pete for clearing so my resistance went down and I agreed to attend one of his workshops. I think part of my reluctance to learn was the feeling that I couldn't work in the way Pete did and I had no intention of driving round the country doing what he had done at my house. The Universe had other ideas for me which would eventually manifest.

"I Am One with the Presence, Power and Consciousness of the Universe and Nothing Can Interfere Now or Ever"

CHAPTER

My Guardian Angel

Within days of attending Pete's workshop, I saw an Angel Workshop advertised in the local paper. Not only was this workshop taking place in my village, but it was actually in the street where I lived. We had only been living in April Cottage for about a fortnight and there was a lovely old house within a walled garden on the other side of the road. It was owned by the council and used for educational purposes which mainly consisted of school groups during the week. I knew there were some adult workshops at weekends, but I had never seen an Angel Workshop mentioned before. Not only that, I hadn't really thought much about angels anyway. I felt a strong urge that I needed to attend this workshop and so rang up and booked in straight away.

There were only a few people who knew about the experiences I had gone through with earthbound souls, mainly my friend Jane and my sister Jayne. Jane had then shared with me all the psychic phenomena that they had experienced in her house but had never been able to sort out, but I'll come back to that later. Jayne had been quite sceptical when I first told her my experiences, but she had suffered lots of health problems and so had been interested to learn about the GS and find ways to improve the energies of her home. Jayne lived up in Yorkshire, but wanted to come on the Angel Workshop with me so came down for the weekend to attend.

The Angel Workshop was quite amazing. It opened up a whole new sphere of information to me. I found it both fascinating and wonderful to realise that we were all surrounded by angels just waiting to be asked for help. I wanted to find out as much as I could and started devouring angel books at the rate of about two a week. I really wanted to communicate with my guardian angel and set the intention to do so. I followed the guidance in an angel book I had read.

Each evening I sat in my little meditation room and followed the steps given in one of the angel books. I was asking to meet my guardian angel and find out her name. It was about the sixth time of trying when I suddenly heard a name very clearly, "Excelsior", in my left ear. I couldn't quite believe that I had heard my angel and asked again. A beautiful soft velvety voice spoke again very clearly and repeated her name, "Excelsior". I was so thrilled and excited but I kept it to myself. I had read in the book that if you think you hear the name of your angel it will be confirmed to you in some way within the next few days. This would either be by hearing the name in a song on the radio or television, or by reading it in a paper or magazine.

The following day I had forgotten about looking for confirmation and later in the evening we had settled down to watch the sitcom "One Foot in the Grave". Victor Meldrew had ordered some garden gnomes but as was usual for him, there was a problem with the order. He stood in his front door shouting out at the delivery man, "What the bloody hell do you call this?" "I ordered one Excelsior"! I nearly jumped out of my skin. This was my confirmation, how incredible.

I began talking with my angel each day. I couldn't see her with my physical eyes, but I could see an image of her in my third eye and of course hear her lovely voice. I bought myself some angel cards and also used these for guidance. Spending time with the angels became a high point of my day and it wasn't long before Archangel Michael came to me and introduced himself. I felt incredible heat as he was talking with me and soon came to recognise this as a sign he had come to speak to me. I kept receiving the message that the angels were going to teach me and I was eager to learn, but had no idea how difficult this was actually going to prove to be. I think I enjoyed about six blissful weeks of communicating with the angels before the lessons began.

"I Am One with All of Life,
I Am Safe at All Times"

CHAPTER

Earthbound Souls

I had learned a technique to rescue earthbound souls working with Archangel Michael and this was successful clearing souls from buildings and also from people. Suddenly it seemed that wherever I went I picked up some souls. I couldn't go shopping into Newmarket or Cambridge without picking them up somewhere and the effect was quite draining to say the least.

I would start out feeling quite well and refreshed and then walk into a shop and immediately feel a heaviness come over me. No matter how quickly I ran out of the shop I had been seen by these souls and they stuck to me in order to be rescued. It was like moths being drawn to a light bulb. My spiritual light was now shining and drawing these souls to me wherever I went. I felt it was part of my 'job' if you like, but by the time I got home my head would be feeling awful and I couldn't wait to get them rescued and off to the 'Light'. If I was near the end of a shopping trip it wasn't so bad, but if I had just arrived in town then it wasn't so convenient. Len also found this very annoying and hated the fact that I had to suffer in order to help these stuck souls.

I could always work out which shop or building the souls had come from and then I would dowse it to confirm and clear the whole building. I gradually worked my way through most of Cambridge and Newmarket to get all the shops I used clear so they became safe areas for me. If we visited another town or were away on holiday I became quite fearful of going into unknown places and so tended to stick to window shopping instead. I think Len was quite pleased about that because in the past whilst on holidays I had dragged him into every craft shop we passed.

Having souls attached to me gave me a headache and made me feel like I was wading through treacle but after clearing myself the relief was immediate. I was therefore very confident about using this skill to help clear my clients and their houses.

When I cleared souls from clients they too would feel the amazing relief and lightness within a day or two of my work. They would notice their house feeling warmer and lighter and their gratitude made it so worthwhile. It was especially wonderful to be able to clear an attached soul from a child. I have many accounts from grateful clients whose little ones transformed overnight into pleasant, happy and co-operative children, having been aggressive, uncontrollable little monsters. Many children with attachments suffer from night terrors, nightmares and suffer from lack of sleep as well.

A lovely lady telephoned me one day having been recommended by a friend. She was a single mum with a fourteen month old baby boy who had cried almost constantly his whole life. He didn't sleep for more than about two hours at a time and both mum and baby were exhausted. The only time he was calm was when they went out for a walk. I told her that I would dowse the house that evening and telephone her the following day. The house had lots of earthbound souls, but none of them had attached to mother or baby. I rescued them from the house and cleansed the energies. When I called her the following day she was overjoyed to have had the first full night's sleep since giving birth to her baby. She said her little boy actually became calm whilst she was talking to me on the 'phone the previous day. It was as if he knew she had found the right help. He was calm during the evening and then had a full night's rest. He was obviously able to see the spirits in the house and felt very disturbed by them. Many young children, and animals, can see spirits clearly whereas we close down those abilities as we grow older.

At this early stage of my new career, I did my clearing work for donations. I never wanted to leave people in a house with earthbound souls as I knew from experience how awful they could make you feel. I also didn't want to set a charge that people couldn't afford having been quoted an unaffordable price to have my house cleared when I was in such a desperate state. I wasn't really sure how to set a price for what I did and so just asked for donations. Mostly small donations came in but at times I had a lovely surprise as in the case of the single mum and her fourteen month baby.

It was about two or three weeks since I had cleared her house and I wasn't expecting to receive very much from her as she was without a partner. I had very little money at the time having left my part time job to concentrate on this work which I felt was my life path. Before leaving my job I had agreed that Jason could go on a school trip to Italy to go skiing. We could pay in instalments and so I felt I could manage it. Without a regular income, however, I had to count every penny. It was a Monday morning and as Jason left for school he reminded me that I had to send in the final instalment of £120 for his skiing holiday by Friday. I had no idea where I was going to find the money so as I vacuumed the carpets I spoke to the angels quite firmly. I told them that

I knew I was supposed to do this work but I did need to earn enough money from it so that I could pay for the weekly groceries at least. I also stated that I needed £120 by Friday!

About an hour later the post arrived and amongst the bills and junk mail there was a letter from the single mum, expressing her extreme gratitude for the help I had given them. She and the baby had now enjoyed deep restful sleep every night since my clearing and she sent me her donation of £120! I dropped to my knees in awe and gratitude. How amazing the Universe is. Sometimes all you have to do is ask.

Earthbound souls were being attracted to my spiritual Light in order for them to be rescued and sent home. This caused temporary headaches and tiredness so you can imagine the possible effect of having a soul attached to you for a number of years. As I mentioned earlier, sometimes when a person dies they refuse to go to the Light because they want to stay with a loved one. They can't bear to leave them and often think mistakenly that they can protect and guide them if they stay. From my experiences I have found this is most common with a grandparent dying and staying with a favourite grandchild. Unfortunately, rather than protecting and guiding the grandchild the absolute opposite can happen. If the soul passes over to the Light then they can visit their loved ones, send messages and signs and give guidance but when they attach to the loved one they cause illness, headaches, depression and more. It can have a devastating and disastrous effect on the person's life which is exactly what happened to a friend's daughter.

I had a good friend, Sally, in the village with a daughter a few days younger than Christian. We had met at antenatal classes and got to know each other at our post natal group. We saw each other frequently when the children were young as they attended play group and school together. My friend's daughter Claire was a very confident and outgoing toddler, the complete opposite of Christian who was shy and never far from my side. If Claire fell over she would get straight back up again to carry on playing whereas Christian would cry and need a cuddle. Claire's confident and outgoing attitude continued through primary school and she had a wide circle of friends. Claire and Christian both attended the same secondary school but by now they had separate friends and so I didn't see her very often. I still got together with Sally a few times a year for a drink and a chat to catch up with each others news. On one of these occasions Sally was telling me that Claire was suffering from IBS and anxiety and had been visiting the doctors but nothing was helping her. She had also now started having reflexology and had decided to visit a hypnotherapist as well as she was desperate to get back to how she was. The next time we met up there had been no improvement at all, but she was continuing with the hypnotherapy. Her problems continued for about three or four years. Due to our busy schedules about a year went by before Sally and I met up again and when we finally got together I asked after Claire. Sally went into far greater detail now as Claire had got much worse. She still had the irritable bowel syndrome but her anxiety levels had increased. She had sudden, violent temper outbursts which she never had in the past. She was also now frightened of sleeping in the dark and needed a night light in the bedroom, something she hadn't needed as a child. She also had all mirrors removed from her bedroom as they scared her. She was often very emotional and said to Sally she wished she could be the happy carefree girl she used to be back in year seven at school. As I listened to Sally hearing all of Claire's problems it sounded like an energy problem. If this was a client talking to me I would immediately expect to find an attached soul. Sally then said she knew exactly when Claire changed, in fact the very week it all started to happen. It was a few days after Claire's granddad had died! I knew then that Claire's granddad had attached to her instead of passing to the Light. I jumped up from my chair and grabbed a pendulum and dowsed and this confirmed my thought. I told Sally and she agreed that I clear Claire that evening. She decided not to tell Claire as it would freak her out. Claire had been the favourite out of five grandchildren.

Having had this soul attached for so long, the improvement was more gradual, but all the anxieties and health problems started to fade and Claire's natural confidence began to return. Within eighteen months she was travelling around the world, partly on her own, sometimes with friends finally being allowed to be herself once more.

"I Celebrate Life with Joy and Gratitude"
Reprinted with permission from *Daily Word*® **UK**

CHAPTER

Lessons

I had been confidently clearing earthbound souls for several weeks and then one day picked something up which wouldn't clear. My sister, Jayne, had been having similar experiences, as well. Although she didn't have clients, being a full time teacher, she did attract earthbound souls herself and had to clear them. We had also discovered that when you had picked up a soul it didn't jump off from one person to another but rather it could split its energies and affect someone else in the same way. So when I picked something up and came home to clear it, quite often it would split and attach to Len or one of the boys as well so creating more clearing work.

Even more bizarre than that, we also quickly discovered that the energies of an attached soul could travel down the 'phone line to affect another person. If Jayne rang me before realising she had a soul attached then it passed to me as well and vice versa. This also happened to me many times when new clients called and whatever was attached to them passed down the phone to me. As I got busier with my work this became a constant problem for a while with me needing to clear myself several times a day.

Anyway, I seemed to have picked something up which I couldn't clear and within no time it had passed to Jayne down the phone so we were both stuck with this uncomfortable presence. For a few days I just kept repeating the clearing procedure but without success. Finally I called in Excelsior and asked her for help. She explained that what I had attached to me was not just an earthbound soul but a dark entity. She went on to say that this entity was afraid of the Light and so would not pass to the Light like an earthbound soul. It still had free will like all souls. She told me I had to learn how to help this entity and clear it in a different way. It needed to go to a 'halfway house', a place of the Light but not in the Light.

That was all the information I was given and I shared it with Jayne. Between us we used meditation, dowsing and information from books to eventually work out how we could clear this dark entity. It was a case of trial and error, testing out clearing techniques daily, dowsing what was right or wrong, until eventually it was successful. I think it took us about three months in all before we got it right and what a relief when it finally went!

The very next day after clearing this dark entity a new client called me for help and my dowsing indicated that she had the same type of dark entity. I tried the new technique out on her and it was successful. She was very relieved as she had been suffering with this attachment for a few years.

My 'lessons' continued in this fashion for about twelve to eighteen months. It seemed that there were all types of dark entity that I had to learn about. This was rather a roller coaster journey with many highs and lows. When something dark was attached I felt very down and desperate and at times even begged God to take my life as I couldn't stand it. However, the angels were never far away and always offered help and support and an assurance that things would get so much better. At one low point I called the angels for help and was shown an image of me standing on top of the world and people coming from all directions over the planet to ask for my help. The people were coming in their thousands and I was helping them all. I thought this was probably my imagination, but as I have progressed in my spiritual knowledge and clearing ability it has proved to be correct. I now do my clearing and healing work distantly all over the world and have helped numerous people.

Whilst not wanting to dwell on the subject of dark entities, it is important to acknowledge their existence. I trawled through so many books whilst I was learning to clear these entities to try and find out more information, but discovered that most spiritual authors prefer to steer well away from the topic. They seem to want to focus only on the Light, which is important of course, but I think some pretend the dark stuff isn't around and so leave many people searching for answers to their problems without success.

My lessons with the angels continued and as soon as I learned how to clear a particular dark entity a new client would telephone and have a similar entity which I would then successfully be able to clear. It was as if the angels had these people lining up in the wings and then brought them forwards as soon as I had the necessary knowledge. Each time that I successfully cleared a client and received their positive feedback was a confirmation for me that I was being taught some valuable lessons and that this was indeed the right path for me to follow. It made all the hard times worthwhile.

Len still found it hard to accept that I should have to suffer when I was trying to help other people despite my explanation that I was learning and the best way was through personal experiences. Our silver wedding anniversary was approaching and we had decided to go on a long weekend city break. I was a bit reluctant to go anywhere due to my sensitivities and the likelihood of picking up earthbound souls and entities but also wanted to have a break away. Len was suggesting possible locations and I was dowsing to see how 'safe' it would be for me. I was dowsing a 'no' to most of the European cities, but finally got a positive to Brussels. It wasn't somewhere we had longed to visit, but was obviously spiritually cleaner than Prague and Rome and some of the other cities so we booked a hotel with good energies for the trip.

The journey to Brussels was a bit of a nightmare for me. Being in large crowds of people was always difficult because some people would have souls and entities attached and they would split off and attach to me. After checking in at Stansted Airport we sat down with something to eat and drink and after a while I could feel the energies getting heavier. I did a clearing on myself and the airport which lightened the atmosphere.

After boarding the plane I could feel the energies draining me again so once the doors were shut I did a clearing on myself and the plane and then felt ok again for the rest of the flight. Arriving at Brussels airport necessitated me doing another clearing and then we boarded a bus to take us into the city centre and as soon as the doors were closed I did clearing again. The repeated attachments to my energy fields were beginning to take their toll and I was feeling quite drained and tired.

The coach dropped us off and we then had to hail a taxi to take us to the hotel. I think the taxi we got into must have had the worst energies of any vehicle in the city. Immediately it felt like arrows piercing my head attacking me. In the enclosed space of a car the heavy energies were concentrated and I felt I didn't have the strength to do anything. We were dropped off at the hotel and after checking in and getting to our room I was finally able to clear the dark energies around me. What a relief it was, but by then I was exhausted and had to lie down and rest.

Len was keen to go out and explore the city whereas I was reluctant to leave the safety of the hotel room but we had to go and find a restaurant for dinner anyway so I shielded myself and we set off. As the weather was fine, we decided that taking an open top bus city tour would be a good way of seeing the sights whilst staying in the open air, which would feel better than being enclosed in if I picked anything up. After the tour we walked in the general direction of the hotel looking for a suitable restaurant. Since following my spiritual path I had become a vegetarian so we needed somewhere with veggie options and I also wanted an outside seating area. I am not sure if it is different now but back then there were very few veggie options on the menus, let alone vegetarian restaurants. We finally found a suitable place to eat so made a mental note of its location to return to later.

Back at the hotel I cleared myself again and we then relaxed in our room with afternoon tea. We decided to go out early for our evening meal to avoid crowds and we arrived at our chosen restaurant with only two or three other tables occupied. We sat on the terrace and had just started eating our meal when a large party of about 30 or more people turned up. I soon felt like I had picked something up so we finished as quickly as possible and returned to the hotel so I could get properly clear again.

Len felt very annoyed that our break was being spoiled by all this energy clearing and he said I should be allowed to have a holiday from this work. We decided that we would visit a park on the outskirts of the city the following day so that I might stay clear for longer. We left the hotel fairly early and went to the metro to catch a train. As the train pulled into the station we were both looking for an empty carriage and luckily the train wasn't busy at all and we got into what looked like an empty carriage. As we sat down we both noticed a tramp sitting on the opposite side, slumped over so he wasn't visible from the platform. I just knew from the look of him that he had some dark entities attached and immediately could feel them on me. I did a clearing and with immediate relief, felt it lifting.

I mentally called Archangel Michael and asked for help. I passed on Len's message that I was on holiday and needed a break from this and asked him what I should do. Archangel Michael then said, "Disguise yourself as one of the Dark Boys". I asked how I should do that and he told me to place a black cloak around me, completely sealed from head to toe to cover up my Light and to place spines on the outside. I did this immediately without question. Just then the tramp opposite sat upright and looked like a heavy weight had been lifted off his shoulders. The clearing had taken effect on him already. The train pulled into the next station and crowds of people boarded the train. I waited but my energies didn't change. Perhaps this cloak was working.

We had a lovely time at the park, visited a museum and had lunch and I was feeling great. Len was surprised I hadn't mentioned anything about needing to clear myself so I told him what Archangel Michael had suggested I do. We went back on the train in the afternoon and it was very busy but I felt completely clear. When we got off at the city centre it turned out that the Gay Pride Liberation Front were marching through the city and there were thousands of people everywhere. People were dressed in all manner of costumes and the city was literally heaving. We had to hold hands so as not to get separated. Unbelievably I stayed clear! I felt normal again. As we walked back to the hotel I ventured into some of the shops and was unaffected by any other energies. I don't know about the Gay Pride crowd, but I felt liberated.

We went out for dinner that evening to a small bistro we had seen the previous day. It had vegetarian options on the menu, but it had no outside seating area so we hadn't risked it before. Now I felt quite confident that I could sit inside and feel clear. We had a lovely meal and enjoyed watching the stragglers from the march walking past in their colourful outfits.

The remainder of our break was very enjoyable and I stayed clear the whole time, even on the journey back home. This dark disguise made life much easier for quite a while. I think I overused it though as I started to get black specks in my aura and Archangel Michael said I had to learn to strengthen my energies so that they were so radiant nothing dark could attach. This also involved a lot of personal inner work to clear all my low vibrations and fears which took time, but did eventually happen. Once all your low vibrations are cleared you find that your shielding and protection will hold. You can be aware of the lower energies without being pulled down by them.

"May I Be Surrounded by the White Light of God's Love, Protection and Guidance"

CHAPTER

Jane's House

It wasn't just me that picked up souls and entities while I was out. Sometimes one of the boys would come back from a night out and have extra company with them that I would need to clear. Quite often it was to make me aware of a venue that needed clearing. Other times Len would arrive home with something attached after being to visit a new client, or maybe with a new type of entity that I had to learn about. I started to question them about their whereabouts so I could clear places in advance and prevent them bringing the stuff home.

By now my friend Jane and her husband had moved to Lincolnshire and I regretted the fact that I had been unable to clear her house and rescue all the souls from the barn fire before she left the village. A lady called Wilma lived next door to Jane and she died a short while after Jane moved away leaving the house to her son who lived in South Africa.

We received a call one day from Valerie, a previous neighbour of ours and friend of Wilma. Wilma's son had contacted Valerie and asked her to arrange for a local tradesman to renovate the bathroom prior to him putting the house on the market. Len had often done plumbing and other odd jobs for Valerie so she trusted him to do a good job

Knowing the energies of Jane's house I felt sure Wilma's house would be similar and full of souls so I dowsed it to check and sure enough it was. I told Len I would want to clear it before he went round there or he would be bringing stuff back home. In those days I always felt I should ask permission from the owners before doing any clearing whereas now I would just ask the Universe and go ahead with any clearing needed. He felt uncomfortable about talking to anyone about what I did so I rang Valerie and told her that I would have to clear the house before I let Len go there, explaining about my new line of work. She seemed quite open minded and agreed she would call Wilma's son and ask his permission for it to be cleared.

Permission was received and so I did a clearing on Wilma's house and invited all souls from neighbouring houses to come forward and go to the Light. The pendulum swung as the souls passed to the Light and then came to a stop. I checked if there were any more and got a no. I then dowsed about the number of souls that had been rescued and was told 53 souls had been rescued and 41 of them had been children. They were now finally at peace following their traumatic death all those years before and Jane's old house was at last clear of all the ghosts.

"Be Still and Know I AM"

CHAPTER

Aliens

Having successfully cleared earthbound souls and dark entities of various types for a number of clients, I was being asked by some of those clients if I would do a workshop to teach what I was doing. I didn't really feel that confident in passing on my knowledge at that stage and also still had quite a lot of fear within me concerning anything from the dark side. However, my sister Jayne had recently been on a Journey workshop with Brandon Bays and had successfully cleared a number of cysts from her breast doing the healing technique taught by Brandon. She was keen to pass on this way of healing to a couple of her friends and so together we decided to run a healing workshop based on the Journey process.

Several of my clients were very keen to come along and together with Jayne's two friends it would give us a group of ten people. Jayne had a client in Wales, Adam, who was keen to learn about dowsing and clearing, but when he heard about the healing workshop he was insistent that he come to that. So our first workshop at my house took place with all good intentions that people would be able to gain healing and knowledge from the experience. Jayne and I asked the angels to make sure that everyone who came was clear as we didn't want any dark entities spoiling proceedings.

Adam asked if he could stay at my house the night before the workshop and we agreed. He arrived to join us for a meal the evening before and he was a very pleasant man. He came with me after dinner to take my dog for a walk and as we strolled along the river bank I felt a sudden sensation in one of my ears which caused a loud buzzing. I felt sure something had jumped onto me from Adam and couldn't wait to get home and clear myself, but didn't say anything to him at the time.

As soon as I arrived home I went upstairs to do a clearing but it didn't shift. I tried a couple more times and then took Jayne aside and got her to try but without luck. We tried a clearing together but still no joy. We then decided to tell Adam about it. He knew he had had something with him for the last three years which no-one had been able to clear, but unfortunately he had omitted to tell us. I think Jayne and I both felt a bit panic stricken. We had a group of spiritual people arriving the next morning for a healing workshop and here we were with some form of entity that we couldn't clear.

I spent a completely sleepless night with screaming in my left ear. Jayne suffered likewise, but Adam said he had slept well. Despite our pleas for help we couldn't get clear and so put on a brave face for the workshop. Half way through the morning a few of the people complained of headaches and we told them that some form of entity had come in with someone and we would have to clear it after the workshop as soon as we worked out what it was.

It was a relief when everyone went home. We had enjoyed the workshop experience, but both Jayne and I felt very guilty that people had gone away with more than they came. Some of the people were completely unaffected, but others started having a terrible time. Whatever this entity was it spread rapidly from the spiritual attendees at the workshop back to their families and friends at an alarming rate. One of the people that became 'infected' from phone contact with Jayne was a very good clairvoyant and could see that these entities were in fact like spiders and were of alien origin. I had always believed in other life forms on other planets, but didn't realise that you got alien entities as well.

Now we had to start trying to find out what to do with aliens which proved to be a difficult task. After suffering with these entities for about three months I decided to contact a well known angel author. She suggested someone called Gerard that could help me. Gerard was a healer and at that time specialised in clearing alien entities. He actually seemed quite excited when I told him the details of the spiders and how they had spread from the workshop. He told me that it was one of his tasks to clear this alien race completely from the planet and he had been waiting for the opportunity to come to him. He started by trying to clear each individual but it soon became clear that this was impossible because they would become re-infected again almost immediately. The spiders had spread so wide amongst us that his guides told him he would have to learn to clear them in one go from the planet.

Gerard also told me and Jayne to let go of all guilt about this. He said each of the people who came to our workshop had agreed on a soul level to come together and be infected with these entities in order that they might be cleared completely from the planet. Gerard worked on how he could complete this task and I think it took about six weeks before they were all finally cleared. The relief was amazing.

The clairvoyant who first identified the spiders told me that now I had met aliens and was aware of their existence I would never need to meet any again. I was relieved to say the least. However, this relief turned out to be short lived.

About six months after our alien encounter a new client rang me one day and told me all of the terrible things going on in her life. I could feel the energies all over me and tried to cut the call as short as possible, so that I could get myself clear and then dowse and clear her. I spent some time trying to clear everything from me. I felt clear eventually and started to dowse and clear the client, but then it seemed to come back to me.

Over the next few days I kept having to re-clear myself, but didn't remain clear for long. A niggling thought kept coming into my mind that I had some type of alien, but I really didn't want to believe that could be the case. Surely I didn't have to come into contact with another alien. After a few more days I decided to contact Gerard and get him to have a look. Sure enough he found an alien and this time it was a chameleon type. He said it was jumping in and out of dimensions, which is why at times I felt it had cleared, but then it jumped back in again.

Thankfully this proved to be much easier for Gerard to clear than the spiders. I was so grateful when it was gone and hoped that was the last of the aliens I had to meet.

In the following months I did quite a lot of inner work and cleared many contracts with beings from past lives. I grew spiritually and my energy fields grew stronger. I had met and learned to clear several more types of entity and was gaining in confidence.

My third alien encounter was about a year or so later. This time I recognised it as alien origin immediately and wasted no time in contacting Gerard. However, by now Gerard had become extremely busy and offered a telephone appointment about six weeks later. He couldn't look at me at all before then.

I couldn't just sit and wait for Gerard to be free to work on me. I needed to get this cleared and felt that the Universe was telling me now I had to learn to do this myself. As had happened so many times previously, this alien was soon with Jayne as well and so we worked together on how to clear it. We discovered information about aliens and also spiritual masters who could help from Joshua David Stone's The Complete Ascension Manual and David Cousins book A Handbook For Light Workers. We had to work with Captain Ashtar and the Ashtar Command and the Cosmic Masters. It all read like science fiction, but I was beginning to realise that it was all quite real.

We created a vehicle using sacred geometry to transport the aliens back to their rightful dimension. We had to get this vehicle through a stargate so they could get back home, but we couldn't work out how to get the stargate opened. So we were stuck at this point.

By now I had stopped telling Len very much about the entities I picked up because he still found it hard to understand that I had to suffer. He knew that I had another alien, but I hadn't shared any other details with him. We were travelling somewhere in the car and had got stuck in a traffic jam when suddenly Len asked if I still had my alien with me. I told him how far we had got and that we were trying to find out how to get a stargate opened. Now Len was a fan of all sci fi programmes. He loved Star Trek, Blakes 7 and Stargate. I had never watched these programmes with great interest although had seen a number of Star Trek episodes. I had never seen Stargate and didn't even know there was a programme of that name. So he told me that in Stargate they used a code and a key to get the stargate opened. I felt I was being given a vital bit of information through Len.

Once home I dowsed and found this was right. So I just asked for the appropriate code and key to be used and the stargate was opened.

The rest of the procedure fell into place and although it was a very long clearance procedure compared to any others I had ever done it finally worked. We had managed to clear aliens ourselves which was quite an achievement.

"Attuned to Divine Wisdom,
I Know What is Mine To Do"
Reprinted with permission from *Daily Word*® **UK**

CHAPTER

Curses

That doesn't sound like a very nice heading, but a curse is just the opposite of a blessing. I had heard about gypsy curses from childhood, but had never experienced anything myself. I was drawn to read a book by Anne Jones called Healing Negative Energies because that was largely what I was now doing and I learned that curses can be muttered under the breath or done with dark intentions in a ceremony.

In her book Anne gave instructions for clearing a curse, working with the angels and the Light using a ceremony with the intention of love. As soon as I read it I knew I would need this information. I had been devouring spiritual books for several years now and would often have a very strong intuitive feeling when a piece of information was important. It would immediately be marked with a sticker for later use.

A few days after reading this I had a new client call me for help with clearing her home, but also because she knew someone had put a curse on her. She knew who the person was and exactly when the curse had been made.

I didn't divulge that I had never cleared a curse before, but only because I wanted to sound confident so she would trust me. The angels seemed to guide me as to what I should say. I told her that I would do a ceremony in my house at an agreed time when she could be alone and undisturbed in her house. I told her to light a candle and call in her guardian angels and Archangel Michael. I then told her that it was important to forgive this person from her heart in order for it to work. I felt it was probably karmic and was the result of her cursing that person in a past life. I also told her to send beams of light and love from her heart to help dissolve the anger and pain in the other person.

My client agreed and said she could forgive and so I conducted my ceremony later that evening with the help of my wonderful angels, Archangels and Jesus. It worked. The curse was cleared and now I had another string to my bow.

I soon came to realise that curses were far more common than I ever could have imagined. Not only did people have curses on them, from sources either known or unknown, but also houses and pieces of land could be cursed as well as objects. I found that where something like witch burning had taken place in a location in the past, then the land and sometimes community was cursed. I successfully used Anne's curse clearing ceremony on many occasions.

The majority of my curse clearings were for objects. These would often be crystals, spiritual statues and figurines or items of jewellery. In most cases they would have been empowered by someone working for the dark side to bring negativity to the owner of the object. I came to call them Negative Power Objects. The negativity quite often took the form of drawing dark entities into the person's house and so once I started work on a property it would soon become apparent that something was constantly bringing more dark entities in.

My first experience of such an object happened before I had learned how to clear them. I was recommended to a friend's cousin to help with all their problems and the house dowsing showed very bad energies so I had started with clearing entities from the building. I began to heal the negative energies in the earth, but each day the house was full of entities again. I asked for guidance about what was happening and dowsed that an object in the house was cursed and drawing these entities in. The more healing I did for the earth, the more Light was coming in and the more this object became activated and drew in greater numbers of entities.

I telephoned my client, Charlie, to let him know this and to ask if he knew what the object in question might be. Intuitively I felt it was something spiritual and something that you would imagine to be bringing you positivity. Charlie came up with three possible items and I dowsed over the phone as we spoke. My pendulum indicated very strongly that it was a Buddha statue. Charlie found this impossible to believe. The Buddha had been made especially for his wife as a gift and she had been told that it was empowered to bring her good luck, health and wellbeing. I enquired as to whether he felt that the family had received any of these things and of course he agreed that it had been just the opposite.

Charlie wasn't sure how to approach his wife with my findings and so I suggested that he remove the Buddha statue to somewhere outside of the house to see if this made a difference. I felt I would then be able to stabilise the energies and continue with the earth healing. Charlie's garage was separate from the house at the end of the lane so he decided to place the statue in the garage, while I continued with the healing. The garage was used for storage rather than for housing the car so it wasn't used on a daily basis.

I carried on with my healing work, checking daily on the energies of this house and it was staying clear. About ten days later I was nearing the completion of the healing when I had a telephone call from a very frantic Charlie. He had gone down to the garage that morning to find something, having forgotten completely about the statue. As he opened the garage door the negativity hit him like a brick wall. He now knew without doubt that my findings had been correct and there was no way he was going to allow this object back into the house.

As I didn't yet have the skills required to clear the object, and it was of a material that couldn't be burned or smashed up, Charlie decided to buy a lead box and encase the statue inside and bury it in the middle of a field somewhere. This seemed the best solution and he contacted me once it was safely buried so that I could clear him and the house and family again. The house healing was then completed enabling the family to move forwards free from the negative empowerment of that statue.

Once I acquired the skills and knowledge enabling me to clear such objects, I subsequently carried out a ceremony on that Buddha statue just so it will be safe if it is found in years to come.

I found myself enveloped in a curse once that I was trying to clear from Jayne. We had been on a workshop together one weekend run by an angel teacher. Jayne had met this lady at a local talk she went to one evening and she enthused to me about how wonderful a workshop with her would be. For some reason I felt reluctant to attend and luckily we had other commitments for the next two workshops that were planned. Part of me was hoping that Jayne would drop the subject but she continued to let me know about future workshops, insisting that it was important for us to attend. Finally I agreed and we sent off our deposits for a weekend workshop in Yorkshire during November. For some reason both Jayne and I had got the dates wrong and pencilled the workshop in our diaries for the week after the actual workshop and only found out when Jayne received a call one Saturday morning asking if we were still coming and just running late. I was miles away of course and so Jayne apologised profusely on behalf of us both and asked if our deposits could be carried forward to a future workshop. The angel teacher agreed and so we booked in for the next workshop in the following January.

The evening before we set off to travel up to Yorkshire for the workshop Archangel Michael appeared at my side. He said I had nothing to fear and he would be by my side the whole time. I thanked him, but thought how strange to say I had nothing to fear. I was going to an angel workshop after all.

As Jayne pulled up outside the angel lady's house, she came to the door to instruct us where to park. She didn't look anything like I had imagined and in fact I saw the word 'dark' written across her forehead. I berated myself for imagining this on an 'angel lady'.

Jayne and I had two totally different experiences at this workshop and I realise now that it was because Archangel Michael was surrounding me. The workshop was very strange, however, and not at all what I would have expected. We were both disappointed after the first day and Jayne didn't want to return for the second day. It was me who insisted we should go back the second day, mainly I have to say, because Len would have been furious if he thought we had driven up to Yorkshire for a workshop that turned out to be useless.

On arriving for the second day, Jayne made a comment, which she later said was completely unplanned and an altercation between Jayne and the teacher followed. Jayne told me afterwards that she telepathically 'heard' the teacher threaten to get her. I won't go into any more details, but the workshop continued as strangely as it had started. Immediately Jayne's life turned upside down and one disaster after another happened. Within a few weeks I had dowsed there was a curse on Jayne and it had come from this woman. Despite several attempts at clearing the curse it wouldn't clear. The more I tried the worse things seemed to get for Jayne and her family. Then the curse seemed to envelop me as well. I began to think that this was a different kind of curse, but seemed to be getting tangled up in a web and then didn't know whether what I was dowsing was right or not. All I could do was pray for help and call in the angels to support and guide me. As always, of course, the help finally came.

"I Fearlessly Follow the Guidance of Spirit"
Reprinted with permission from *Daily Word®* **UK**

Spiritual Response Therapy

I had made friends with Marlene a few years before when I met her at one of my herbal training days. Marlene had suffered health problems and found the herbs to be hugely helpful. She was passionate about looking after the body with herbs and nutrition. Our herbal teacher had arranged for a kinesiologist to visit and give us a talk and demonstration using our muscles to test what herbs would be beneficial. At the break Marlene started telling us about her problems with sleeping and headaches and how someone had visited and placed a crystal on their electricity box to see if this helped. I immediately mentioned geopathic stress and dowsing and suddenly the whole group were intrigued and questioning me about earth energies. I got my chart and pendulum out and dowsed the homes of several of the people there.

Unfortunately for the kinesiologist, the people were more interested in hearing about the earth energies then, than what she had come to talk to us about, but it was obviously meant to be. Most of the group came home with me to find out more and I was subsequently able to heal all their houses.

It was the start of Marlene's spiritual journey and I passed on knowledge and information and did dowsing and clearing on her many times. I tried to persuade her to come and learn dowsing with me, but like me in the early days, she resisted learning until eventually she gave in and attended a Spiritual Response Therapy (SRT) course in Wales. She enthused about it and recommended that I should do this as well. Travelling to Wales seemed out of the question to me so I didn't pursue the idea.

It was about eighteen months after this that I was being affected by the curse on Jayne when Marlene called to tell me that her SRT teacher from Wales was coming to Peterborough with a colleague to run a course and would I be interested in attending. As she spoke I knew intuitively that this was the answer I had been praying for. I said yes immediately despite not having the £250 fee, but knowing it would be provided somehow.

I sent off my deposit of £25 and asked the angels to help me manifest the remaining £225. I had total faith that this would happen and within a week a new client had contacted me for healing work on his home and work place. I dowsed his addresses and told him I worked for donations so he promised to post me a cheque. The following day his donation arrived and guess what, he had sent £225! My course had been paid for.

Learning SRT gave me a huge acceleration in growth of consciousness. It is one of the most amazing therapies I have ever come across. As it is dowsing based and I was already a confident dowser, I took to it like a duck to water. SRT is all about clearing negative programmes that have accumulated in the Akashic Records from past lives. The effects of clearing these programmes can be incredible. At the end of the first day I spoke to the teachers, Peter and Mike, about the problems I was having and Mike promised to look at me that evening. I actually had the most awful experience that night and felt under attack. The following day I reported back my experiences and Mike did a full clearing on me that evening. However, I still felt terrible and knew there was something else. At lunchtime on the third day I told Peter and Mike more details about the Angel Workshop and what had happened to Jayne. They both dowsed and meditated and then discovered that the 'Angel' teacher was a close soul mate of both me and Jayne and they needed to research and clear a specific life between the three of us. As Peter's pendulum swung while he cleared the life I felt tremendous pressure lift off me immediately. It was just dissolved and I felt light and free once again. I knew without doubt that this therapy worked and was important for me to use on my clients. Peter and Mike dowsed that the 'Angel' teacher actually worked for the Dark Forces and they did their best to clear her, but said it would be up to her to make a conscious choice to change. Jayne and I had to clear contracts we had with her from past lives together and after that the curse she had put on Jayne was cleared. Normal life, if you can call it that, was resumed.

One of the most important aspects I learned with SRT was the way of connecting and working with the Higher Self. Your Higher Self works with a committee of angels and guides in spirit to do clearing and healing. The clearing procedures I had learned under the instruction of the angels now became redundant with the exception of the special alien clearance. My Higher Self committee was able to clear all other types of earthbound souls and entities much more quickly than previously had been possible. It seemed I had learned a long way in order to help my understanding but now could work with more speedy techniques. SRT uses a chart showing all the types of discarnate in varying degrees of darkness so it is easy to identify what type of discarnate is affecting a building or person and then ask for it to be cleared. I discovered that my Higher Self can clear some aliens but not all. Whenever I come across them I just ask whether they can be cleared easily with HS or not. Sometimes I have to ask the angels to open up a temporary portal to the appropriate dimension that the aliens are from and then get them escorted back 'home' and occasionally I have to use my special alien clearance.

I worked on a property once that had four different types of alien entities as well as other discarnates in the form of earthbound souls and various types of dark ones. It was interesting how I came to work on the house as during the time Len and I were looking for a building plot we often passed a site of derelict ruins in a prime position. It would have been far too big a plot for our budget, but we always admired the site and wondered if it would be built on one day. Sure enough the time came and the site was cleared and a new building started. By this time I had learned a lot about energies and came to realise that there was some strong blocking energy at this site. There were a number of delays during construction and the project was on going for a number of years.

Each time we passed by I felt there was some dark energy and wished I could clear it for the owners to help them. As it was a private house you couldn't just clear it without permission, but I longed to do so. It was a huge property with stunning views and I knew how much better it would be if the energies were healed as well. Well they do say, 'be careful what you wish for' because sure enough the opportunity arose for me to do just that.

One of my clients, Sarah, worked at a natural health clinic in Suffolk and often referred clients to me when she felt their houses needed clearing. I had cleared and healed the clinic for her and the other therapists as well. Sarah rang me one afternoon to say there was a horrible smell at the clinic which had come in with someone the previous day. They had tried various cleansing methods, but the smell wouldn't budge. They were still seeing clients and so had to pretend the drains were blocked as a reason for the awful stench. Sarah asked me to check the energies and do any clearing to find out what it was. My dowsing indicated an alien presence which I was able to clear with my Higher Self. When I called to let Sarah know she said the smell had gone completely, but she was worried that it would return if the same client came back for more treatment.

She knew that three ladies had attended the previous afternoon and so gave me the names to identify the source of the alien attachment. I dowsed who had the alien with them and it was the lady who Sarah had suspected. Sarah and the other therapists at the clinic had decided they should inform the client and ask her to agree to being cleared because they were anxious that she may become a regular attendee and they couldn't risk this energy coming back again. Sarah volunteered to telephone the client and try to find a way of explaining this to her. Not easy, as you can imagine, unless you are very open minded. Sarah then told me where the client lived and it was in the new big house that I had wished I would be able to clear one day.

Amazingly the client was very receptive to the idea of being cleared, mainly because she had an awful smell in her house which she had been trying to get rid of unsuccessfully for some time. She rang me immediately to arrange to be dowsed and cleared. I was still at this stage picking energy up over the phone and so it took me a while to get myself clear after speaking with her. I cleared huge numbers of souls and entities of all types before I started on the aliens. I found four different types of alien, one of which could be cleared by my Higher Self, two sorts that needed temporary portals opening to their own dimensions and the fourth type which needed my special alien clearance.

It was quite a mammoth task to get the property cleared of all the entities and then dowse the earth energies that needed healing. It seemed strange that all these aliens were trapped at the site and I asked some questions which revealed they had been trapped since the 13th century. I also dowsed they had been drawn there accidentally by a wizard doing inter galactic experiments! The owner of the house was thrilled to find the awful smell had disappeared and was very interested in my findings. I began the earth healing work but she called a couple of days later to say the smell was back. I re-dowsed and cleared the house again, finding all the same type of entities back. It was only then when I talked with her further that I discovered her husband's mother lived in the same village and he visited frequently and it seemed the entities had been going back and forth with him. His sister also lived in the village and the same thing had happened there.

I had to clear all the four types of alien from each of the three houses which was quite exhausting and a huge relief when it was finished and the houses remained clear. I then proceeded with clearing all the other types of discarnate from the three houses and did full earth healing on each. It certainly needed doing and will have lifted the energies for the whole village.

I was subsequently invited over to the big house with Len one morning for coffee and it was wonderful to see inside the property and visit the site that we had admired for so long. I also realised that when I first wished I could clear it I wouldn't have been able to as I didn't have all the skills needed. I longed to be able to clear it and the Universe delivered it when the time was right.

"Abiding in the Presence of God,
I Am Clearly Guided"
Reprinted with permission from *Daily Word*® **UK**

CHAPTER

13

Earth Healing

After being taught about the clearing of earthbound souls and all the different types of entity over a period of about eighteen months or so I was in a position that I could dowse people's homes, clear the psychic presences, but could only suggest purchasing neutralisers to eliminate the Geopathic Stress. There were various gadgets on the market and many of them were not able to do what they claimed. They were also quite expensive. I had found one such gadget which seemed to work fairly well, but it was a lot of money and I became aware that many people living in bad energies were also experiencing financial difficulties and so buying such an item was often out of the question.

I often prayed to the angels that I wished there was a way of being able to heal or clear the detrimental earth energies so that people could improve their health and wellbeing, but I didn't actually think this was possible.

A friend came to visit me one day with a book he had just finished reading called Healing Sick Houses by Roy and Ann Proctor. He left the book with me saying it had been written for me and this couple did exactly what I did with dowsing but they also healed the energies. I read the book avidly within about four days and knew then it was possible to heal geopathic stress. I looked at Roy and Ann's web site to find out how I could learn this skill, but the courses were a long way away and quite expensive for me. I decided I could try contacting them and find out if they would teach me how to do the healing as the rest I already knew.

However, before I could email them my post arrived with a letter and floor plan from a previous client. She was a therapist and had moved into new shared premises along with three other ladies. They were extremely sensitive and wanted me to dowse the building. I dowsed it on my charts and got readings for the level of GS and vitality. I use a scale that runs from -5 at worst to +5 at best, working on a 180 degree dial. I also dowsed for psychic presences and asked about the percentage vitality, or life force energy, of the building. The building dowsed at -4 for GS, there were psychic presences in the building and the vitality was only 10%. Ideally this wants to be at least 75%.

I dowsed the floor plan of the building with a ruler and pendulum and marked on the two rays of GS that I found, noting their strength and direction. I asked permission to rescue the souls and was then able to send them on to the Light. I then began to wonder if it was possible for me to heal these two lines of GS so I invoked my Guardian Angel and started asking her questions. She told me that I could heal it, so I asked about where the healing should go in, what words I should use and whether I had to invoke any particular Angel, Archangel or Spiritual Master. My questions were all answered and I was told that I should work with Archangel Sandalphon, the Archangel for planet Earth.

I didn't actually do any healing but just asked about how it should be done. It was a Friday afternoon and so I decided I would telephone my client on Monday morning and see if she would like me to do a trial healing on her premises. As I returned home from my usual dog walk after breakfast on Monday there was a message on the answerphone from my therapist client. She said they had all come into work that day and the whole place was feeling different. She wanted me to dowse it again and see what had changed.

I found my pendulum and chart and re-dowsed the property. I couldn't believe how different it was. It was now registering +1 for GS and the vitality had risen to 70%. I couldn't understand what had caused such a change and then it suddenly dawned on me that through my intention and questioning the angels had actually done a large amount of the healing work to show me that it could be done. Having such sensitive people in the property they were able to confirm for me that a huge shift had taken place.

I felt very excited as I telephoned her back to tell her what I had been dowsing about on the Friday and the two sets of readings that I had taken. I offered to now do a healing session with intention on the premises and she naturally agreed. With one healing session my first property was healed and the customers extremely grateful. I was over the moon that this was actually possible and waited with excited anticipation for the next property to come forward.

As had happened with my lessons on souls and entities, the Universe brought forward properties with different types of detrimental energy so that I could learn how to heal and rebalance them with the Earth. The second property came forward about three weeks after I healed the therapists' premises. I set out to work as I had previously and although initially the energies started to improve they reverted back to the original reading after two days. I persevered with the healing, but after a week I was still back at square one and couldn't understand why.

I sat quietly in my meditation room and called in Excelsior and asked her to help me understand what was happening. She showed me a picture of the floor plan I was working on with the two rays of GS plotted and where they crossed she showed me a column, rather like a concrete pillar. She said the healing energy was being sent into the line of GS but when it reached this column it rebounded out again. She told me this was a negative energy block. It had been caused originally when something painful happened to either man or animal on that site and the Earth absorbed that pain. Gradually over the centuries the Earth had become saturated with so much pain and negativity that it was now pushing this back up as it was raising its own vibrations towards ascension. As these blocks come up from the Earth they literally block the life force flow around a property. This in turn can block health, relationships, jobs and finances amongst other things.

Excelsior told me I must send in the angelic healing energy directly into the column of negative energy to dissolve it completely and once this was done the rays of GS could be healed as I had done before. I followed her guidance and the block dissolved and the healing then progressed to give a significant change from the original reading. The client at this property was also very sensitive and gave me immediate positive feedback once it was completed, although interestingly she had experienced several ups and downs whilst I was learning about the blocks.

Just about every property since then that I have dowsed has had several of these negative energy blocks. Many houses have a dozen or more and it is always essential that they are dissolved completely before continuing with the rest of the healing, or it will not hold. Lots of people ask me where they can read more about these blocks, but I haven't found mention of them yet in any books.

"I Contribute to Peace in the World Through my Thoughts, Words and Actions"
Reprinted with permission from *Daily Word*® **UK**

Sacred Geometry

During the start of my journey I was guided to read books constantly. In fact I devoured them at the rate of about two a week. I found myself preferring books to television and if I sat down I had to start reading. My soul was pushing me to read and learn as much as I could in as quicker time as possible. I came across the term Sacred Geometry in various books that I read and started working with Sacred Geometry in a number of the clearances that I developed.

Although I read and understood that Sacred Geometry was powerful, I didn't actually experience it for myself until just after I started learning how to heal the detrimental earth energies. We were planning a holiday in Spain, just Len, me and Jason, as Christian was going away with his mates for the first time. Jason found a lovely apartment in Mijas and I dowsed it as being a +3 for GS and vitality was very good as well.

In the past when going away, we usually took a set of the GS neutralisers with us to help enhance the energies, but this time as the property dowsed so high I decided not to bother. Len wanted to take them as a precaution, but I persuaded him that it wasn't necessary as if there was any GS I could heal it once there.

We arrived at the apartment well after 11:00 pm so basically went straight off to bed. There was one main open plan room with a kitchen area, dining area and lounge. At the far end of the lounge was a bed settee consisting of two separate single beds, one underneath the other. The double bedroom was just off this room. Although I dropped off to sleep I woke up again fairly quickly with a bad head and feeling like I had GS in my body. I tossed around in bed, gradually feeling worse, until eventually I could stand it no more and got up around six in the morning.

I crept across the bedroom trying not to disturb Len but he could tell there was something wrong. When I told him I was suffering the effects of GS he was quite cross because I hadn't let him bring any neutralisers. I assured him that when I felt better I would dowse the apartment and heal any GS.

I made myself a cup of coffee and took some painkillers as my head felt so awful. I sat down on an armchair in the very centre of the room being careful not to wake up Jason. Len got up about five minutes later and also came to get a coffee and then Jason stirred. He asked what we were going to do that day and Len started to say that I was feeling ill so we would have to wait until I felt better. I had only been up about ten minutes, but was starting to feel great improvement already. It would normally have taken a couple of hours at least to start recovering from the effects of GS. I didn't want to move from the chair. I was experiencing a rather pleasant sensation which felt like all the negative energy inside me was being washed out. I told Len and Jason that I was starting to feel better and so there was no problem making plans for the day.

With that I laid my head back onto the back of the armchair and was amazed to see a very large six pointed star on the ceiling directly above me. It was like a plaster rose that you often see on ceilings in older houses. It was in the centre of the ceiling and this chair was placed directly under it.

"Oh my goodness", I exclaimed, "I can feel the energy coming from that six pointed star and it's clearing the GS from my body". Jason said quickly, "Let me feel it", and stood under the star, but was disappointed he couldn't feel anything. I sat there for another half hour feeling healing energy pour over me until I felt refreshed and ready to start the day.

I drew out a plan of the apartment and located a line of GS just outside the bedroom, but obviously close enough for me to feel. I asked permission to heal it, but this wasn't granted. I couldn't get a clear answer as to why not, but deduced from this that I was supposed to sleep under the six pointed star whilst here. There was no way I could stand trying to sleep in the bedroom so that night we pulled the other single bed out and positioned it under the star. I also dowsed that though the apartment measured +3 overall, the bedroom was only +1.5 but the presence of the star in the living room increased that room to +4.

I spent the rest of the holiday sleeping under the star knowing that it was no accident we had come to be there and that it was another lesson for me. Len was not so thrilled however, as I spent the holiday sharing a room with our fourteen year old son whilst he slept alone in the bedroom. I knew that I had to incorporate the six point star into my earth healing work and was looking forward to experimenting when I returned home.

I remembered whilst on holiday having read about stars in David Cousin's 'Handbook for Light Workers' so I looked up about the six point star after we got back. Sure enough, he said it could be used to transmute negative energy from the earth where something violent had happened like a murder, or other tragedy. I dowsed that I should use the six point star on my house and was quite excited about the wonderful energies this would create.

I placed a six point star above the roof of my cottage and filled it with Divine Light and waited to see what happened. The following morning I woke up feeling negative energy in my body and found a negative energy block had come up from the earth and through my side of the bed. I healed this immediately and cleared the energy from my body. The energies in our cottage were good when we moved in and there had never been any negative blocks before. I couldn't believe this had anything to do with the star so came downstairs for breakfast. As I sat at the breakfast table in my usual chair I started to feel my body fill up with negative energy again. I dowsed a negative energy block had risen up under my chair, so I healed it, but felt this was just rather bizarre. After walking the dog I went into the study to do some emails and found another negative block had risen up under my office chair. I was starting to feel very confused. The only thing I had done was place a star over my house filled with Divine Light and yet I was feeling strong negative energy in the house wherever I sat.

I went into my meditation room and called in Excelsior to ask what was going on. She showed me a picture as she often did to explain things. I saw my cottage with the star above it and the power of the energy in the star was drawing negative energy from the earth from all the neighbouring properties up through my home and as they came into the star they were transmuted.

My dowsing indicated that I had to place the star underneath the house so that it could continue transmuting negative energy from the earth around, but not allowing it to come up inside the house. Once I had the star placed in this way the energies in the house remained stable again and I started to use this technique on the properties I healed. I started to realise that once I healed a property in a particular town or village, another two properties in the same area were brought to me, often completely unrelated to the first one. My angels told me that the power of having three stars in close proximity increased the clearing power dramatically. There are now thousands of these stars all over the world helping to clear the vast amounts of negative energy that man has been heaping onto the planet over the centuries.

Another problem that I was taught how to correct using sacred geometry was negative vortexes. These are swirling vortices of energy that bring dark entities into this dimension. You can have positive vortexes which are fine, but the negative ones need to be cleared and closed off. A particularly sensitive therapist contacted me one day for help in clearing her house. She had the gift of sight, so could see what was going on and had been struggling to keep herself and her house clear for some time. She told me there were three vortexes on the property, one in the living room and two outside in the garden. I had never come across the term before and so it involved me doing daily clearings and trying out various techniques to stop them opening up again. I think it took about three or four weeks before all the information I needed came to me so that I could clear and close them off permanently. The process involved me using five, six and twelve point stars, working with the Archangels Michael, Metatron, Uriel and Sandalphon. It was a great relief to the client when everything finally remained calm and within a year she was able to sell her house and move, which she had been trying to do for a several years. Quite often the Universe will not allow you to move from a place until it is healed. We make contracts before incarnating, agreeing to bring about healing to houses or areas and then are held there until we fulfil our agreements.

Just after successfully clearing those vortexes, I had a number of others brought to me which I was able to deal with quickly. Jayne, my sister, also told me that she had been invited to go with a healing group to a well known beauty spot where a number of people had been drowned when the waters rose quite suddenly. The group planned to go and meditate at the area as the leader of the group had been told there was a large negative vortex over the site. They were hoping that as a group they could do healing to correct the vortex. Jayne was anxious about going along with hoards of dark entities swirling around so asked me to clear it before they went, which I did. The group sent healing in when they got there which will have added to my efforts. I have not found that many vortexes around, thankfully, but far more common are portals. Again you can have Light portals which are positive, but also dark portals which bring in dark entities from other dimensions. These are far more prevalent.

As with many of the things that I learned from the angels, I had to learn about portals through my own experiences. I had got a number of interested clients coming to one of my dowsing workshops, amongst them a powerful clairvoyant, healer and dowser called Paul. Paul had been told by his guides that he must come and thought that he had to meet me for some reason as he didn't need to learn to dowse. A week before the workshop I was planning to visit a Mind Body Spirit Fair near Cambridge and Archangel Michael told me to go and see the medium at the fair, a lovely lady named Maureen Flynn. Michael told me that she would have a message for me. I had never actually had a session with a medium before and was quite excited. I arrived at the fair as soon as it opened so that I could make an appointment with Maureen and rushed straight away to her stand. A notice on the table explained she was held up in traffic and hoped to arrive within the next half hour. So I wandered past her stand and saw the Kirlian photography being set up. A Kirlian photograph will show up a person's aura and I had had such a photo taken a number of years beforehand so thought it would be good to have another taken and this would fill in the time until Maureen arrived.

I had my photo taken and then waited to see one of the readers who would interpret the aura's colours. When she saw my photo she was quite amazed. She said there was a spirit with me, so close it was touching my face. She wanted to know if I could feel it, but I said I was aware of Lightness around me and only noticed spirits that were earthbound. She seemed to be rather gobsmacked and could only keep repeating that this spirit had a strong message for me as it was so close. I then told the reader about Archangel Michael telling me to come and see the medium here that day as she was going to give me a message. The reader suggested it was important I show Maureen the photo.

I left the photography stall feeling rather tingly with anticipation. Maureen Flynn had now arrived and was seeing her first client so I signed up on her list for the next available slot. When the time finally arrived I introduced myself and told Maureen about Michael's message and showed her my Kirlian photo taken a short while before. "Well, you have an Archangel overshadowing you", she said. I asked her which Archangel it was and her guides told her Archangel Metatron. I asked what the message was, but she could get nothing. Instead, my dad came through, along with my grandmother, my uncle and several of my dad's friends. They all seemed to be having a party up there which was a great comfort, not only for me, but also for my mum, aunt and a number of their friends when later I told them about my session. Although Maureen tried a get a specific message nothing else came through.

I felt quite honoured to have Archangel Metatron overshadowing me although I had no idea why. I felt extremely safe and protected and assumed all would be revealed in time. The day of my workshop arrived the following week. As well as those already booked, one lady asked if she could bring a friend along who was staying with her at the time. The friend could dowse already and was interested to see my way of working. I agreed happily and so we all gathered in my dining room to start the workshop. I always check and clear people attending a workshop before it begins to prevent them bringing souls and entities into the group, so we were clear to begin with. It all started well until we called in Spirit and then suddenly I could sense some entities around. Paul was able to see them jumping around from one to the other, as they tried to evade being cleared. After several attempts, and with Paul's help, we got the room and everyone clear and were able to proceed.

At lunchtime a few people decided to go across to the pub and I asked them jokingly not to bring anything back. When we all gathered back in my house again I immediately felt some souls around so started the afternoon session with a clearing, obviously calling in spirit to help. Suddenly, things went downhill and entities were streaming into the room. Paul could see a portal had opened up in the middle of the room. I had never come across a portal before and felt a bit fearful although trusted that things would get cleared. After all, I had an Archangel overshadowing me so how could anything negative happen. This portal kept re-opening and allowing all sorts of entities in and I think it took about an hour to get everything clear and stable again. The workshop timetable went completely awry as there wasn't time to do everything planned and we all decided against any more meditations.

By the end of the day I was completely exhausted and felt too tired to dowse what had happened or why. Paul rang me once he got home to see if I realised what had been going on. He said one of the ladies in the group was working for the dark side and that every time we called in Spirit, she was bringing in the dark ones. He said she had anchored a portal into my room which I needed to clear to prevent it opening up again. He also told me to place a pyramid around the house as a form of protection. I felt quite upset to think this had been allowed to happen and couldn't understand why Archangel Metatron had allowed it. I dowsed the spot in the floor of my room and sent in healing and placed a pyramid around the house as protection.

I fell into bed and slept deeply and trusted that the matter was sorted. Just after waking the following morning I was sitting in my meditation room going through my daily spiritual practice when I suddenly felt a portal had opened in the house. I cleared the entities and closed it and cleansed the house through and felt clear again. I placed the pyramid protection back around the house and hoped that it would hold. Unfortunately, later in the day I had to repeat the procedure when a portal opened again. I asked for help and guidance from my angels and Archangel Metatron but nothing came to me. I rang Paul to see if he had any more advice, but he couldn't tell me anything else. It seemed his part had been played in helping me during the workshop and giving me the beginnings of the protection.

The next morning the same thing happened whilst I was doing my morning practice, so I added a bit more into the pyramid structure around my house for protection and again asked for some help. Later in the morning my dear friend Caroline Izzard rang me. She had been a client with ME and I had healed her house and dowsed many things for her. She was also a wonderful clairvoyant and healer and had helped me many times over the previous few years with her clear insights. She was ringing because she had been to a shop in her local town that she had visited many times before, but on this day she had felt the energy to be extremely negative. She had seen a huge portal in the shop bringing lots of negative entities into the space. Her guides told her to ring me.

I then told her about the events of the previous few days and she thought we were supposed to work together with the help of Archangel Metatron to develop a protection to stop such portals arriving. Caroline assured me she would meditate on the problem and come back to me.

She was told that we had both been incarnated together in Atlantis where we had worked with Sacred Geometry and we had been drawn together in this life to remember that work and to put the powerful pyramid protections in place around the Earth where needed. So we worked together again sharing insights and information as it came to us. Each day a portal opened in my house which I would feel within seconds. I would dowse a little more about the protection needed and knew that when eventually we had it exactly right, it would hold and stay clear.

It took almost three months for that to happen. What a relief it was when during the first week of January 2005 the pyramid protection held and no more portals came in. Caroline put the pyramid structure around her local shop and this also stayed clear. Suddenly, portals began opening all over the UK and in many countries abroad. For the next six months I was using the new protection technique every week and started to plot the pyramid protections on a map in case any patterns emerged. Also, during this period there were a number of 'lunar standstills'. I am not an expert in astrology at all, but I am interested in the subject. I read an article written by Jonathan Cainer where he said the effect of these lunar standstills was to increase the width of the ley lines all over the planet so that by the summer solstice they would cover the entire globe. I was intrigued by the meaning of this and as I had a ley line running through my cottage I checked its width and started to notice it increasing around April of that year. I had to rebalance myself with the energies of my home on a daily basis and the ley line increased to about 325 feet in width by the middle of June. I made myself comfortable in my meditation room on mid summer's day to listen to a meditation CD by Drunvelo Melchizadek called the Unity Breath Meditation. However, part way through I was no longer able to hear Drunvelo's words and I was being shown a different picture. I was seeing the whole globe with the ley line energy covering the entire planet and then I saw all the pyramid structures I had been placing over the previous few months light up as pinnacles of brilliant light. I then saw the Christ Consciousness Grid over the Earth, to which the pyramids connect, and saw this Christ energy travelling down the pyramids and into the ley lines of the planet. This energy was then being used to awaken many souls over the whole world.

I realised then the importance of remembering this sacred geometry formation and the reason it had to be in place in sufficient places ready for this particular day. The ley lines gradually returned to their original size over the following few weeks. I also started to find that many smaller ley lines had appeared and were running through nearly all the properties I dowsed. Since that time the amount of portals opening has drastically decreased and I am probably only required to use the pyramid protection a few times a year.

It also then dawned on me that the lady who came to my workshop and caused the first portal was actually bringing me a gift and helping in my spiritual growth and learning even though she was working with dark energies. It must all have been part of Archangel Metatron's plan and it was only because I had to keep clearing the portals from my own home that I persevered with learning the protection. If a client had asked me to do this I would probably have given up.

"I Learn and Grow Through Every Experience"
Reprinted with permission from *Daily Word*® **UK**

Manifestation

During my spiritual journey I read many times about manifestation and began to realise that we are actually all manifesting all the time without even knowing that is what we are doing. We are all co creators with the Divine and all manifestations begin first with a thought. Our thoughts create which is why we should observe our thoughts in case we are creating things that we would rather not have. I didn't start manifesting with intention until a few years ago, but have manifested many things during my life prior to this.

We bought our first house together in Bar Hill, Cambridge, just before we got married in 1977. We were both living near King's Lynn in Norfolk, but Len's job had moved to Cambridge so that is where we had to live. Our mortgage offer was based on my salary at my job in King's Lynn and our budget was very limited so it was more a case of what we could afford rather than choosing what we wanted but we managed to find a little, brand new end terrace house with a reasonable garden and a garage in a block nearby. We purchased it for the grand sum of £9,350. The house builders were running a scheme whereby you could have £500 reduced from the price if you did all the decorating and tiling yourself. This enabled us to buy the house and we had great fun choosing colours and tiles to decorate our first house. Within eighteen months we found we could afford the mortgage easily as my salary had increased considerably since working for a company in Cambridge. We had replaced our old second hand appliances for new and we decided that whilst we could afford it we should look for a new home in a village further out from the city. We started to make a list of all our 'wants' as having now lived together for a couple of years we knew more about what we wanted from a home than we did when we bought out first. Our list was quite long and detailed and we were expecting to find something that ticked all the boxes. Our house was put on the market and within a week we had a buyer so we started looking in earnest. In the first week of our search, the details of a semi detached house with three bedrooms in the village of Burwell came through the post. It was in a country lane, in a small group of six houses around a courtyard setting. It looked quite charming in the picture and ticked nearly all our boxes. The only exceptions were that it had oil fired central heating and Len had specified gas, and it had a garage in a block whereas Len wanted a garage next to the house. Because of these two items it was put in the discarded pile, even though I felt very drawn to it.

Every weekend and some evenings after work we viewed properties all around Cambridgeshire, but nothing came close to what we were looking for. Our buyers started to push us to get the legal proceedings moving and so we started to feel pressured into finding something quickly. We had been searching now for about four months and began to wonder if we were being too choosy. The agent then took us to view a house which actually ticked all our boxes. It was lovely, but I felt it wasn't right. The agent and Len enthused about all its good points and

I had to agree and yet I definitely didn't want the house. I couldn't explain why, but my gut instinct was telling me 'no'. I didn't even feel I could tell Len how I felt because I wasn't able to give any reasons why I didn't want to live there.

It was decided that I should go and make an offer on the property on the Monday and so I went along with it feeling there was no other option. I walked along Regent Street at lunch time, feeling very uneasy as I approached the Estate Agents office. I made our offer to the agents and felt terribly sick as I did so. I had never experienced such a strong intuitive feeling before and didn't know how to deal with it. The lady in the Estate Agents was bubbly and excited for me as it was such a beautiful house. I left the agents and strolled back to the office feeling quite down and silently praying that our offer would fall through. I prayed hard each day, willing for something to happen that would stop us buying this house. On the Thursday morning our agent rang to say he had some bad news. My heart actually skipped a beat with anticipation. He said the owners of the house had lost the property they were moving to and so they were taking their house off the market. He apologised profusely and said he would see what else he could show us over the weekend. I felt like the weight of the world had been lifted off my shoulders. The knot in my stomach released and I felt so relieved. Len was very disappointed when I told him the news, but I assured him we would find something soon. The agent took us to see two properties just on the market the next Saturday morning, but they were both awful. We drove home feeling quite depressed and I began to feel guilty that I had caused us to lose the other house. However, when we got home the post had come and there were details from another agent of a house for sale in Burwell. It was the house I had liked the look of in the first week of our search and now it seemed it was back on the market again at a reduced price. I rang up immediately and arranged to view the following day. It seemed an encouraging sign that this house was available again and I felt that it was meant to be for us. As we drove into the courtyard setting at the front of this house we both loved the look of it. There was a small green in the centre with five weeping silver birth trees blowing softly in the breeze. The fronts of the houses were adorned with pretty hanging baskets and as we approached the house we had come to view, noticed that a beautiful climbing rose was blooming over the archway of the side gate into the garden. By now the fact that the garage was a few yards from the house was not so important. We also decided that oil heating could be changed to gas, so apart from that it did tick all our boxes and we felt very much at home as soon as we went inside. We made an offer the following day and proceedings went ahead enabling us to move there in the middle of summer. It turned out to be a very happy family home where both our children were born.

So we did manifest what we wanted then without realising it. We almost went ahead buying another property, but my intuition guided me to manifest that house out of the way and then bring forward the right house at the right time. I now believe that the spirit of a house draws to it the people it wants to live there, so a house chooses you rather than the other way round.

Christian manifested his first car, again without actually having the intention to do so and having no conscious awareness of the fact this was possible. We had only been living at April Cottage for a few months and he had recently had his 16th birthday. I didn't even realise he was thinking about a car yet a while, but one day when I was driving him back home another vehicle passed us in our road and he remarked that it was the sort of car he would like to buy. I was quite astonished as it was a customised Astra van with purple, lilac and blue patterned paintwork and dark tinted windows. A few days later I noticed it parked in a driveway a few doors down from our house, but didn't think much more of it. At the time I had a part time job in a children's nursery as a lunch time assistant and one day a nursery nurse, called Hannah, was transferred to our toddler room. Whilst chatting to Hannah, I discovered she lived just a few doors from me. I enquired as to whether the purple and blue van belonged to her family and it was her brother's. What's more he wanted to sell it. I told her that Christian would love it and to find out how much her brother wanted for the vehicle. Christian had got £600 saved up so that was all he could afford to pay. The following day Hannah told me her brother wanted £1,200 for the car. I said immediately that it was outside of Christian's budget and broke the news to him that evening. I then forgot about it, but Christian often saw the car drive past his bedroom window and was obviously setting his sights on owning it and wishing it was his, all it actually takes to manifest! About five months later Len and I were returning home from shopping one Saturday morning and as we passed Hannah's house saw her brother sticking a 'For Sale' sign into the purple blue van. We slowed down to see how much it was and surprisingly it was now £600. We told Christian and he went with Len straight away to have a proper look at it. They took it for a test drive and managed to knock him down to £550. Christian returned home with the biggest grin on his face which I think stayed there for some time. He had manifested the exact car he wanted within his limited budget with considerable ease.

When we decided to sell the house we had built on the old slaughter house site, it was a sudden decision and due to the energies and my extreme sensitivity to them, we wanted to find something quickly. My main priority was to move into a house which was free from geopathic and geopsychic stress, but I also wanted to have some of the lovely features that we had in our current home such as exposed beams, inglenook fireplaces and a large kitchen. I just asked the Universe to help me find a house that fitted the bill in Burwell where we could be happy. I looked through the houses for sale in the local paper and if I liked the sound of the property I dowsed over it to check the energies. We only actually went to view two houses and decided on the period cottage as firstly it dowsed as a +3 on my chart, which meant it had no geopathic stress and secondly the vitality was very good as well. When we viewed it there were lots of hidden surprises which you didn't expect from the outside. It had original exposed beams and two inglenook fireplaces and a fabulous kitchen space with vaulted ceilings. I say kitchen space because it actually had two kitchens, one in dark oak and another in pine with an open archway separating them. The current owners had split the cottage in two to provide a granny annexe, but had now returned it to one space without refitting it. This didn't worry us in the least with Len's skills and I knew that he would be happier if he had some projects to undertake. The cottage also had two staircases and we decided that we would be able to take one out and create another small room upstairs. Our initial thinking was another bathroom, but after we moved in, Len had the idea to make a small meditation and dowsing room for me. Although we found the cottage within a couple of weeks of asking the Universe to help us, it took about eight months to sell our home. However, I am sure the spirit of the cottage had chosen us and the Universe was also working to help us and so the cottage remained on the market ready for us to buy once our house sold. So you often just have to ask for what you want and as long as it is in your Highest Good then the Universe will deliver.

If what you ask for doesn't manifest then there could be something blocking it, very possibly you are blocking it yourself. Many of us are running self sabotage programmes in the subconscious or immediately after asking for something send out a negative thought to stop it happening, so cancelling out what we have asked for. A lot of these programmes can stem from past live experiences, but you also do have to become aware of your thoughts and change them if need be. It can help tremendously if you get into the right vibration when making affirmations about what you want to manifest. Imagine that you already have received what you are asking for and as the Universe sees your vibration of joy and happiness it will reflect back more of the same towards you so enabling the manifestation to come into being all the more quickly.

I have now managed to manifest two cars quite successfully. When I had my 50th birthday a few years ago Len bought me a personalised number plate. When your surname only has three letters in it this is quite easy to do and not very expensive. He tried to find my log book to get the new plate registered to my car, but he couldn't find where I kept it so gave me the plates saying we could get it registered to my current car unless I was thinking of changing the car and then wait and have them put onto a new one. I hadn't really thought much about changing my Renault Clio but once he had put the idea in my head I began to wonder whether it might be a good time to change it. I decided to think about it for a couple of weeks and then, as I was walking the dogs down by the river bank one lunch time, I suddenly decided I wanted to change the car. I told the angels that I wanted to find a new car, another Renault Clio, but this time with power steering, alloy wheels, low mileage, automatic and either black or blue. I also specified that it must be safe and reliable and told them my budget. I thanked the angels for finding it and asked them to alert me to where and when to look for it. The following morning our local paper arrived and as I flicked through the pages over breakfast I suddenly felt that my new car was already for sale. As I got to the car section an advert seemed to jump out at me. In bold letters I saw "Automatic Renault Clio, Black". I read the rest of the information and it fitted exactly with my request. I found my pendulum and my dowsing confirmed that this was the car the angels had found for me. I arranged to go and see it the following day with Len, but I already knew that I would be buying it. We took it out for a test drive and it was lovely. I decided that I wanted to get £1,000 for my old car, but the garage would only offer me £400 in part exchange. I told him what I wanted and he laughed at me. I said that I would sell my car privately and so completed the paperwork and arranged to come and collect the new car the following week. As we left the garage owner said if I managed to get £1,000 for my car he would give me a job as a car salesman! I placed an advertisement for my old car in the local paper, offering it for sale at £1,100 in the hope I would manage to get my desired amount. Not only did I sell it to the first person to come and look on the first day it was advertised, but he offered £1,000 and I accepted it. I could also have sold it about five times over!

The angels found me the perfect car that fitted the bill and it was safe and reliable for the four years that I kept it. We decided towards the end of last year that we needed one of our cars to have a bigger boot so that the two dogs and luggage could be fitted in more easily when we went on holiday. We had started going on walking holidays with the dogs in different parts of the country and it was a squeeze getting everything we needed into the car as the dogs filled the boot on their own. I don't have very good spatial awareness and have always felt more confident driving smaller cars, so I wasn't sure what sort of car I should get. I asked the angels to help me find the right type of vehicle, again specifying all my requirements. We went along to a large car salesroom in Cambridge to test drive a few different vehicles and see what I liked. I only drive automatics so that immediately limited our selection. The car salesman suggested a Nissan Qashqai and took me to look at one. I hadn't heard of a Qashqai before and thought it looked too big for me to drive, but because it was higher than ordinary cars I had a much better spatial awareness when driving it. I dowsed that this was the best type of car for me and so again enlisted the help of my beloved angels to find a car with all my requirements. I also dowsed that I would find it on the internet and it would be within 40 miles of my home. Len kept checking every few days despite the fact that I told him it wasn't available yet. After about two weeks I had the feeling it was now up for sale and my dowsing confirmed this. Len logged in and we soon found the car I had manifested. We drove along to see it and also got offered a good part exchange deal on my Clio, so the angels had helped my manifestation yet again.

You can of course ask the angels to help you with small purchases as well as larger items. I needed to get myself a new winter coat for dog walking a few years ago. It needed mainly to be warm and waterproof, but I also wanted a hood and large enough pockets to take all the paraphernalia I take with me on walks. I was happy to pay a reasonable amount for a good coat but when I started looking they seemed to be an extortionate price. Several were priced in the region of £250 and more. I went out looking for a coat to various shops on about three occasions without having asked the angels to help me. After the third attempt at finding something it dawned on me that I should ask the angels for their assistance. I gave them my list of requirements and actually saw a mental picture of the sort of coat I wanted. I pictured a brown waxed and warm lined coat with two large patch pockets and a warm lined hood that fitted my head perfectly. My existing coat had such a large hood that when I put it up it came over my eyes so was impossible to use whilst walking two dogs. I also wanted it to be less than £60. I thanked the angels but wasn't sure where else I could go and look for this coat. About an hour later I remembered that they sold country clothing at a large garden centre south of Cambridge. I thought it would probably be very expensive, but we had a drive out there the following morning and found the small clothing section in the shop. I saw 'my' coat immediately. It was exactly what I had imagined and fitted perfectly. The price tag was even better – just £29! It is still serving me well today.

"I Create the Life I Desire"
Reprinted with permission from *Daily Word*® **UK**

CHAPTER

Angels

Never go shopping without your angels! They can help you find exactly what you are looking for, at the right price and in the quickest possible time. This is really helpful if you are going out to buy new shoes or an outfit for a special occasion. I tell the angels what I am intending to buy and ask them to guide me to the right shops. This works every time without fail. If I am Christmas shopping I tell the angels before I leave home for whom I am buying presents and ask them to talk to the guardian angels of those people to find out what they would like. I also ask that I find the items quickly and easily. If my mum comes on a shopping trip with me she is always amazed at how quickly we manage to find and purchase all the things we wanted. It makes shopping trips much less tiring. Always remember to ask the angels for a good parking place as well. They never mind helping you no matter how trivial your request. Len is very proud of his car and anxious that it doesn't get knocked by someone else's car door in a car park so he always asks for an extra wide space and he nearly always gets one. If there are no wider spaces then I ask the angels to protect the car with a shield to keep it safe from knocks.

The angels will always come to you when you ask. They don't interfere, so have to be invited to help, but are always waiting in the wings and hoping that they can be of service to you. You can also, of course, ask angels to help other people. Ask the angels to guide and protect your children, family members and friends. If you see an ambulance or fire engine rushing past, ask angels to help whoever is in need and also to help the emergency services that are responding. I had a call one afternoon just as I was about to leave the house. Something urged me to pick up even though I was in a hurry for an appointment. It was a friend calling me from hospital with a request that I send her some healing. She had undergone an operation and was feeling very low and depressed. Her mind was swirling with bad memories from her first marriage and she kept crying and couldn't sleep. I told her I would be happy to do so and she was too emotional to talk anyway. As I was on my way out I just asked that thousands of angels were sent to her immediately to help in whatever way they could. I thanked them and left for my appointment. The rest of my day and evening was so busy that I forgot to actually send any healing to my friend. She called me later the next morning to thank me for what I had done. She said within two minutes of calling me she fell into a deep restful sleep. She woke briefly for dinner but then slept soundly the whole evening and night and felt a new person free from worries the next morning. I told her that all I had done was to call angels to help her but she thought a miracle had been worked on her.

It's so important to tell your children about angels when they are young and listen to your words. If they can learn to ask their angels for help and assistance it will bring them enormous benefits. When I first started working with angels Christian was a teenager and thought it all a load of nonsense, but Jason was about twelve and seemed interested to learn and understand more. Jason then went through a few years of disbelieving until he had his first car when he was sixteen. There was a particular part of the car which had to be removed. To do that, the front wheels had to come off. Len had bought the new part feeling confident that he could replace it himself but found that the wheel nuts were rusted on. Len and Jason started working on the car late one afternoon in the autumn when I happened to be going out for the evening. They both took it in turns to try undoing the wheel nuts, but they were stuck solid. Gradually it got dark and then started raining. Jason was holding an umbrella over Len as he crouched on the drive trying to shift the wheel nuts, getting more and more frustrated as time went on. Len eventually told Jason that he thought they would have to give up and Jason said, "If mum was here she would ask the angels to help". "Ok you try asking the angels then" replied Len. "Only if you do too" said Jason. Len agreed that they would ask together and so they both silently asked the angels to help. Len bent back down, picked up the spanner for one last go and 'hey presto' the wheel nuts came off without any trouble. Suddenly, two sceptical males were astounded at the result of their request. I think the angels respond in that way to help people believe.

After an end of term break from university I was driving Christian to the park and ride bus stop outside the city centre so he could get a bus to the train station for his journey back for the new term and exams. There was a stream of cars in front of us crawling along very slowly and Christian was anxious he would miss his train. I decided to drive him all the way to the railway station, but he still thought we would be too late because of all the traffic lights we needed to drive through. I told him I would ask the angels to turn them to green for us. As we approached the first set of lights they changed to green and we proceeded to the next set. These also changed to green and we sailed on to the third set which did the same. Christian then wanted to know what I had done and I told him the angels were helping us and that if he was supposed to be on the train we would get there in time. Seeing the traffic lights all change before his eyes sparked his interest and he was open to hearing more about how the angels could help in his life. I suggested he ask them for help in his exams and that if he felt a mental block at any time he could ask the angels to help him recall all the knowledge and information stored in his brain.

I got Christian to the station in time for his train and it wasn't till he returned home after his exams that he told me how much help he found the angels gave him. He had been surprised and delighted by the angelic assistance and started using the angels to help in other areas of his life as well. Not only that but he started telling his friends about angels too which for a nineteen year old male is quite something.

When clients come to me with problems, I often suggest that they hand the problem over to the angels and ask for the Most Benevolent Outcome. If the problem is related to the energies of their home, or past life blocks, then I can clear and sort it out, but sometimes there is not much I can physically do. One such client, Daisy, called me one day after being referred by a therapist. Her list of problems was extensive. She had suffered all types of health and financial problems which started when the neighbouring property built an extension and it was discovered that both the houses were built on an Anglo Saxon burial ground. The building work disturbed the stuck souls and it seemed everything went wrong in her life. Apart from the health issues there was an on going court case which was causing her terrible stress. Daisy and her husband had a business which had been closed down and they were taking another party to court, but it had been dragging on for three years and the other party kept stalling. I took down all the details and dowsed the energies and did extensive clearing of the souls in the vicinity. There were souls attached to Daisy and her husband and one of her dogs which I was able to clear and then restore all their auras. I healed an energetic pattern and cleared a curse on the area and dowsed the earth energies to be healed. When I rang Daisy a couple of days later to discuss my findings I had forgotten about the court case, there had been so much else to dowse with the energies of the house. She asked what could be done about the court case so I told her to hand it over to the angels and ask for the Most Benevolent Outcome. "How do I do that", she responded. I told her to literally just ask, as if talking to a person next to you, explaining that the situation is causing extreme stress and give it to the angels to sort out, followed by thanking them and then letting it go. They were due in court again the following month.

I proceeded with the healing of Daisy's house and then about ten days later she rang to say they had received a letter from the other party, completely out of the blue, offering an out of court settlement. The sum offered was not as much as they would have received it they had won the case, but it was enough to pay off the debts and expenses and, best of all, it meant the stress of the situation was removed. She felt very relieved and was now totally converted to calling on angelic assistance whenever needed. So the angels had brought about the Most Benevolent Outcome for Daisy.

I generally talk to the angels in a soft gentle way, offering gratitude always, but on occasions I have shouted a command to them and seen the immediate results. I have been an animal lover all my life and always had a dog in the family. I will tell you more about my animals in a future chapter, but we bought a golden cocker spaniel puppy in February 2010 and called her Honey. She was utterly adorable and got on really well with our black Labrador, Tia. It was the week before Christmas and Honey wasn't quite a year old. It was bitterly cold with snow lying on the ground. The river had been frozen for several days and it remained about -8 deg during the mornings, never getting above freezing. I was taking the dogs on their usual morning walk around a field adjoining the river. There was a bank between the field and the river which I sometimes walked along, but it felt a bit more sheltered to remain in the field that day. During the previous couple of weeks, whilst the weather had been wintry, I had twice seen an image in my mind of Honey in the middle of a frozen river with just her head and front legs above the ice, trying desperately to get out. Each time I saw the image I thought it was a negative thought that was in my head and I didn't want to give it any energy so dismissed it quickly. In hindsight I realised I should have dowsed whether I was being shown a premonition of something that was going to happen and asked if it was possible to change it, but this didn't cross my mind at the time. As we walked that morning both the dogs ran up onto the bank and seemed interested in something in the river. I called them back and they returned to me for a treat, but both ran off again to the bank. It was then that I saw the same image of Honey in my mind for the third time and felt it was a warning. I called them to me with the intention of putting Honey back on the lead, but she was so quick and my fingers so cold that I fumbled trying to hook her lead on and she raced back up to the bank and this time carried on down the other side.

Tia remained on top of the bank, but gave me a look of concern. I felt panic rise up inside as I ran to the bank and as I reached the top was dreading what I would see. The exact mental picture was there before me in real life. The entire river was frozen, except for a thin channel in the centre, and Honey had obviously raced over the frozen water curious to see the moor hens and sea gulls wading on the ice and had fallen in. She was desperately scrabbling to get out and I called her, but couldn't imagine how she would get sufficient grip on the ice to pull herself out. Thoughts raced through my mind of losing her before she had even reached her first birthday. She had beautiful long fur which I thought would be getting water logged and could drag her under at any moment. I called out loud in a commanding voice, "Angels get her out now". It was as if an angel put a hand under her bottom and pushed her up because suddenly her back legs came up and she was running back to me. I scooped her up in my arms thanking the angels with all my heart for saving her.

She was soaking wet and as we made our way home her fur began to freeze. I wrapped her in a towel when we got inside. Slowly, she dried and warmed up and was none the worse for wear. I did some healing on her and dowsed that it was a past life trauma programme that was repeating and so I was able to clear it for her. I dowsed that if I had cleared the programme previously she wouldn't have gone through the experience. It taught me a lesson to take note of premonitions in case they are warnings of things that can be prevented.

Honey is a very sociable friendly dog and loves to meet other dogs. She expects them all to be as friendly as she is and I don't think the possibility of an aggressive dog ever entered her mind. Len was with me one Saturday morning walking the dogs around another field adjacent to some stables where they keep guard dogs. I had never seen the guard dogs out of their pens and often felt sorry for them as they would howl when we walked past. The owners didn't live on the site, but came to feed them when they attended to the horses. As we passed the entrance to the site that morning the owners were there, but we didn't think any more of it. We were about three quarters of the way across the field when we suddenly heard a woman shrieking out the name of one of her dogs. Her voice sounded panic stricken. Len looked around and then told me the guard dogs were coming after us. I glanced round and then froze to the spot. I have a fear of dog fights after witnessing a couple when I was a child. I saw three German Shepherds and a Collie heading towards us at an alarming rate, baring their teeth and snarling. They were all focused on Honey. Tia was standing near me, also frozen to the spot. She is a very gentle dog and never wants confrontation. The owners called again and the Collie and one of the others returned to their master leaving a black German Shepherd and a three legged black and tan one still chasing us.

Honey didn't seem to sense any aggression from them and actually started to move towards them. I thought Honey wouldn't stand a chance and so with a loud voice I commanded "Angels Protect Them Now!" Len then took a stance and raised one arm and shouted "STOP". Amazingly, the black dog obeyed. The three legged dog was much slower and hadn't looked so menacing, but then caught up and cut in between Len and the black dog and jumped on Honey who let out a squeal. Miraculously, the two guard dogs then turned and ran back to their master. Len picked Honey up and checked her over and initially couldn't find any injuries although later that day we found a small single puncture wound. We stood still for a while. I was shaking, my heart thumping in my chest. Len said he had heard me call the angels and was sure they had saved Honey from being mauled to death. He said he couldn't imagine how she would survive with two such aggressive dogs heading to attack her. We both felt very grateful to the angels for their intervention. I found out later that unlike us, dogs don't have their own guardian angels. You can however ask that an angel is assigned to your dogs to protect them from all types of danger and they will then remain with them all their life.

Several years ago I began training to be a crystal healer and the course consisted of five modules each taking place on a separate weekend. A friend of mine had enrolled and did the first weekend, then enthused to me about it and I felt sure it would be a good thing for me to do. I contacted the teacher and she was happy for me to join the course as long as I did module one at the start of the following course. I agreed to this and when the time came I went along on my own to do module one. The teacher said I was probably supposed to meet someone on this course and this was the Universe's way of bringing it about.

During the practical session in the afternoon I was teamed up with a man called Chris who owned a crystal shop in Bury St Edmunds. He gave me his card and offered me a discount if I bought any crystals from his shop. At that time we didn't go shopping into Bury very often, but about three years after the course Len and I had started taking dancing lessons, learning ballroom and Latin, and needed to buy some dancing shoes. Our dance teacher recommended a little shop in Bury St Edmunds and so one Saturday morning we drove into the town to look at dance shoes. I also wanted to buy two crystal angels as presents for babies. One was for a client who had managed to conceive after several healing treatments with me and the other was for a great niece. I decided to look in the crystal shop although I wasn't going to ask for a discount so long after the course and didn't even know if Chris would remember me.

We arrived in the town centre by 9:30 am but the dance shoe shop hadn't yet opened so we made our way to the crystal shop. We walked in and I recognised Chris immediately but he didn't show any recognition of me. I asked if he had any angels and he pointed out a few dotted around the shelves. Len spotted an unusual one made from Malachite and quite intricately carved, but I told him it didn't look right for a baby. Len suggested I buy it for myself though and I decided I should treat myself so kept hold of it whilst looking for the two gifts. Once I had made my selection I placed the angels on the counter. Chris said, "Oh, you're having three angels" and smiled. He then asked me if I was an angel healer by any chance. I then reminded him that we had met in the past on the crystal course and that I was indeed an angel healer. He then asked if he could share with me what had happened to him that morning and I was happy for him to do so.

Chris said he didn't know very much about angels or do any work with them but that morning in meditation the Archangel Metatron had appeared to him asking that he facilitate an Angel Day in Bury St Edmunds. He asked for confirmation of this request and Archangel Metatron said "Three Angels. An Angel Day, at the Angel Hotel, on Angel Hill". Bury St Edmunds is a lovely old medieval town with lots of references to the name 'Angel' on various lanes and roads. It has a cathedral and the ruins of the old abbey amongst the Abbey Gardens. Chris agreed to the request and came out of the meditation and proceeded to get ready and opened the shop up at 9:30 am still pondering the message from the Archangel and wondering how it would come about.

I then walked into the shop at 9:35 am, the first customer of the day, and purchased three angels. I told Chris that this was definitely a confirmation sign for him and I gave him my card and told him to let me know when it was arranged as I would love to attend.

About a week later I received an email from Chris informing me that two other angel healers had been introduced to him and they were forming a committee to start arranging the Angel Day and inviting me to join them. I didn't generally get involved with committees and part of me wanted to decline his offer, but I knew in my heart that this was something I had to be involved in so I responded immediately that I would love to be part of it. Through various synchronistic events Chris met several other people in the following week until there were nine of us in total and we had our first meeting together in the room above the crystal shop.

We shared our various ideas about what form this event should take and then ended our first meeting with a meditation, inviting the angels to guide us and bring about exactly what was required. In the meditation I saw a huge golden angel hovering above us in the centre of the room, radiating out golden light and there were nine golden ribbons coming from the angel, one attached to each of us. As this was our first meeting and we didn't know each other I didn't feel confident enough to share what I had seen so kept it to myself. However, the next day one of the group, Jo, sent us all an email telling us about her meditation at home after our meeting where she had seen a huge golden angel with golden feathers floating down around her. I then decided to share what I had seen in the meeting. I knew it couldn't be my imagination as Jo and I had both seen a huge golden angel.

We all did some research to find out about possible exhibitors for our event before meeting up for the second time. I mentioned to the group that my sister, Jayne, did channelled angel batik paintings and would love to exhibit at the event. I passed around some photos of her work and everyone agreed it would be lovely for her to have a stall. One of the group asked if Jayne could channel the golden angel so that we had a batik hanging of our own angel and also if she could find out the angel's name. When I asked Jayne she agreed it would be lovely and the golden angel appeared to her the same night. Jayne began the channelled art work and asked the angel for her name. Although angels are genderless she definitely had feminine qualities and exuded pure joy. Jayne was given the name Excelsior. Jayne sent me a text and asked me to dowse if she had got the name right. When I saw the name on my phone I couldn't believe it. I had never shared the name of my Guardian Angel with anyone, not even Jayne. I was also confused. I grabbed my pendulum and dowsed about the name and was told it was correct. I asked why this angel had the same name as my own Guardian Angel and was told that my Guardian Angel worked under the Archangel

Excelsior and had taken her name. The Archangel Excelsior then spoke to me and told me that she had brought the group together and that all nine of us had contracted to do this prior to incarnation. She said there was a huge angelic presence in the town of Bury St Edmunds, but it was not being utilised and our event was required to bring in the Light and anchor this angelic energy into the town.

By way of confirmation, the following day I received a package of charcoal discs that I had ordered on the internet about ten days previously. They had the name of Swift Lite Charcoal Discs but as I opened the package the first name I saw in large print was EXCELSIOR! This confirmed to me the information was correct and I shared it with the group at our meeting later in the week.

I had healed the Angel Hotel in readiness for our event, but at our third meeting it became apparent that this venue would not be large enough. However, adjacent to the hotel there is a beautiful Georgian building called The Athenaeum and this proved to be the perfect location. I did my earth healing on this building as well and Archangel Excelsior then requested that I heal the whole of the Abbey Gardens site. This meant there were three of my six pointed stars in close proximity to bring the Divine Light firmly into the area. Not by accident I'm sure, but the Michael and Mary Lines run through the Abbey Gardens. These ancient Ley Lines start in Cornwall and can be traced through various locations, including the Abbey Gardens where they touch or 'kiss' before heading out to the coast in Norfolk.

It was a very busy time for the group as all the organisation got under way until our first very successful All Angels Day event took place. The batik hanging of Excelsior had been put in various shop windows in the town to advertise the event and there was much interest amongst the townspeople as to what it was all about. The Athenaeum was buzzing and the vibrant energy well and truly anchored the Light.

A local dowser had tracked the Michael line through the building at the start of the event and at various times throughout the day and it expanded considerably by the time the day drew to a close. This was another confirmation of the success of the day, if we were in any doubt about it. Our contract was completed by that first event but our group continued for several years introducing the topic of Angels to many more people.

During the organisation of our first event Archangel Excelsior appeared to me often in meditation usually encouraging me and with gratitude for being involved with the group. One winter's night I was woken by her and she wouldn't let me go back to sleep. She didn't say anything but was just in my mind. After a while I checked the clock and it was 2.00 am. I really wanted to go back to sleep but try as I might I couldn't get Excelsior out of my mind. I then began to wonder why she was keeping me awake. I am diabetic and sometimes get low blood sugars at night so it crossed my mind that I should do a blood test in case I needed to eat something. I didn't feel like my blood sugar was going low but thought I better check it anyway. I generally take my test kit upstairs to keep by my bed at night, but on this occasion I had forgotten and left it downstairs. I decided I had better go down and do a test. Our stairs lead down into the kitchen which is a long room with a brick floor and a breakfast area near the bottom of the stairs. There is a vaulted ceiling with velux windows in the roof so with moonlight and street lamps it is always light enough to see at night without switching the light on. My test kit was on the breakfast table so I did a blood test, but it was fine. I turned to go back upstairs when I noticed the moonlight reflected on the kitchen floor and realised there was water on it. Then I turned the light on to see that water was actually pouring out from under the kitchen cupboards beneath the sink. The water had come across to almost the other side of the kitchen and had progressed down the length of the room, nearly reaching the breakfast area where the dogs were sleeping peacefully in their beds. There is then an opening into the lounge which is carpeted.

I shouted for Len to come quick. He turned off the stop cock and we then spent the next hour mopping up all the water with bath towels. Len found a pipe had come off under the sink and the water would have continued to run. If I hadn't been woken by Excelsior and come downstairs the flood would have progressed through the entire kitchen and lounge, ruining the carpet for sure. We went back up to bed just after 3:00 am and this time I was allowed to go back to sleep.

During a talk on angels that I went to once I found out that we all have our own angelic name. When we find out what it is we can use it to feel empowered during spiritual work and meditation. We can actually choose to use it as our name if we like. I tried out the meditation when I got home and I heard the name "Free" but this didn't sound like it was the whole name. I attempted the meditation a few days later and this time I heard the name "Freedom". This sounded more complete but I felt there was still more to my angel name. On my third attempt I very clearly heard that my name was "Wings of Freedom". That sounded right but I asked for confirmation of the name. Immediately, I saw in my mind's eye an aeroplane flying in front of me with a wavy banner trailing behind it saying very clearly "Wings of Freedom". I laughed out loud; the angels have such a sense of humour sometimes. I stood up and raised my arms up in the air and exclaimed "I Am Wings of Freedom". I felt like I grew to ten feet tall and an extreme sense of power filled my being.

I started running Angel Workshops myself a few years ago so that people could learn all about angelic help and find their own angel names as well, which are often just ordinary sounding names. One lady attended my angel workshop and although she had been a healer for several years hadn't known anything about angels. She practised at her home in the country and also at a clinic near London. The work at the clinic was increasing and so she had decided to rent a flat nearby and work at the clinic for half the week and the remainder in the country. She was having difficulty in finding a suitable flat so after the angel workshop she decided to ask the angels to sort the problem out for her. She went on a viewing weekend a short while later to see what the angels had found for her. The clinic was near to the docks and she wanted to be in walking distance of the clinic if possible. Unfortunately all the flats she viewed were terrible and at the end of a long day was feeling quite disillusioned. She was about to set off home and decided to buy a drink from the shop before doing so. As she went into the shop her eyes were drawn to a card in the window advertising a small boat for sale. The name of the boat actually drew her attention as it was the name of a town in Germany where she was born. This was not the normal sort of name you gave to a boat. The asking price was more than she could afford but as she travelled back home she began to wonder about the possibility of living on a boat whilst working at the clinic. She rang a friend who was more knowledgeable in such matters and he said before buying a boat she had to find a mooring. She decided to ring the marina near the docks to find out if there were any moorings for rent and found out that there were two currently available, one small and one large. The following week she went back to have a look at the moorings and to her amazement the little boat with the German name was tied up in the small mooring. The owner of the Marina told her that the boat was for sale privately and would be gone soon leaving the space vacant. She said that she was actually looking for a boat of that size but couldn't afford the asking price of this boat. He said that in his opinion the boat had been very much overpriced and he thought if she was interested should offer only half that amount. He also said the owners were moving abroad and needed to sell quickly. He was holding the key for the boat so fetched it for her to have a look inside.

The little boat really fitted the bill for her so she asked the angels to help her to buy it at an affordable price. She rang the owners and offered half the asking price as the man at the Marina had suggested. They said no straight away but took down her details anyway.

She felt rather disappointed but a couple of days later returned home with some shopping to find a message on her answerphone from the owners of the little boat saying that if she was still interested they would accept her offer. She had a client arriving soon for a massage so there wasn't time to call them then and in any case she needed to sort out finances. She told her client all about the little boat and how she hoped she would be able to borrow some money from the bank quickly and he asked her how much she needed to borrow. When she told him he said if she could pay it back within a year he would have the sum transferred to her bank account later that day and wouldn't charge any interest on the repayments.

So by the following weekend she was the proud owner of a little boat, renting the mooring in the marina adjacent to the docks where her clinic was, so being able to relax and enjoy her own space after treating her clients. She was so grateful to the angels for their help and I was fascinated to hear her wonderful story.

"May You Always Have An Angel By Your Side"

CHAPTER

Animals

In the last few years I have done some training in animal communication. Apart from learning from some human experts, I have also had guidance from Shandy, a dog we owned for fourteen years who has now passed over.

We currently share our home with two dogs, a black Labrador/ Collie cross called Tia Maria, a golden Cocker Spaniel called Honey, a huge beautiful cat called Tango and the most recent addition being two male Marginated Tortoises called Gilbert and Digby. I have been an animal lover for as long as I can remember and my parents bought a Staffordshire Bull Terrier cross puppy when I was about two years old. He was brindle with a white swirl on his chest and two white front paws. His name was Butch and he was a wonderful pet and playmate when we were growing up. He was very gentle and obliging with our games. Jayne and I often dressed him in old baby clothes and wheeled him around in our dolls pram. We had a younger brother called Brett and we would put Brett into one of the prams and Butch in the other and then wheel them both round the garden. Butch had the ability to smile and he loved to sit on a small chair watching out of the lounge window. When we came home in the car, pulling into the drive, we would be greeted by Butch's smiling face and wagging tail.

Even though I loved Butch to bits, I still wanted lots more pets. I used to tell my parents I wanted to be a vet when I grew up although what I really wanted was my own little zoo. Butch was a typical terrier so his instinct on seeing anything small and furry would be to chase and kill it. So despite my pleadings to have a kitten, guinea pig or rabbit, I was always met with the same response that it wouldn't be fair to Butch. My cousins lived in Chalfont St Giles and whilst we were staying with them during the summer holidays one year we found out that their next door neighbour owned a tortoise. It was a large tortoise that roamed around the garden. The owners had drilled a hole in the back of its shell and tied a long green cord through the shell which was attached to a stake at the other end and sunk into the edge of the garden. Knowing now how sensitive a tortoise's shell is it must have been extremely painful to have had a hole drilled into the back of it. However, the thought of having a pet tortoise set me pleading for one as I thought Butch would probably not be bothered by such a creature but the answer was always the same.

One summer holidays Jayne and I were feeding our friends' pet rabbits whilst they were on holiday. We walked down the lane each morning with a fresh supply of greens for the rabbits and watched them for a while munching through their breakfast. On one such morning we could hear frantic chirping nearby and noticed a fledgling sparrow, obviously distressed and calling for its mother. We thought it must have fallen from its nest and was now abandoned and in danger from cats and dogs so we decided to rescue it and take it home. We found an old bird's nest in our hedge and put this into a cardboard box to make a lovely home for our new little pet who we called Chirpy. We fed Chirpy on cereal mashed up with milk and kept his box on top of the coal bunker outside our bedroom window where we could keep him safe out of the way of Butch. A couple of times each day we would let him wander around the garden, trying to teach him to fly by persuading him to jump from the little garden wall and always ensuring Butch was shut in the house at those times. We looked after Chirpy with tender loving care for the whole summer and I was very reluctant to go back to school in September. We left our mum with strict instructions about letting Chirpy out in the garden during the day and to make sure Butch was kept inside at those times. I think we had only been back at school a week when we came home one rainy afternoon to find Chirpy's box empty. When I asked mum where he was she had forgotten he was still in the garden and Butch, of course, had been out a few times during the day. I searched the flower beds and borders and then eventually found little Chirpy, wet and cold and very dead. He had fallen victim to Butch's terrier instincts without a doubt. I sobbed my heart out and was furious with mum for being so careless.

My dad often went away on business trips abroad and always brought us presents when he came home. A short time after we lost Chirpy dad was going away on such a trip and asked what sort of present I would like him to bring me back. I said I would like a rabbit and he said he would see what he could find. I had a real rabbit in mind and tried to hide my disappointment when he came home with a fluffy blue rabbit toy. However, a few weeks later I had a wonderful surprise when he came home from work one day. Dad worked in the film industry and did film editing and directing and often made commercials. I don't know what the commercial he was making at the time was actually advertising, but it required three white rabbits. Dad had asked one of the runners to get three white rabbits and hutches for the filming. When it came to the end of filming he asked the runner who owned the rabbits as they could now be sent home. The runner replied that they were the owners. He had been unable to borrow any so had purchased them from a pet shop. Dad asked the rest of the crew if anyone wanted to re-home them, but nobody was interested so dad brought them home. I can still remember clearly the evening he came in with the baby rabbits in a box. I think I was about seven years old at the time and I felt my dreams had come true. Dad said Jayne and I could have one each and we would give the third one to John, the little boy next door. John was about a year younger than me and he called his rabbit Peter after the Beatrix Potter character. Peter lived to a ripe old age which is more than can be said for Snowball and Snowflake, the names we gave to our rabbits.

Snowball and Snowflake shared a large hutch on top of the coal bunker outside our bedroom window, exactly where Chirpy's box had been. This was the safest place to keep pets so that Butch couldn't get near to them although I am sure he was well aware of their presence. We loved letting them out to run around the garden when Butch was shut indoors and their pure white coats were so soft. I think we had only had them for about a couple of months when one Saturday morning my dad cut some rhubarb for my mum to make a crumble and decided to give the leaves to the rabbits for breakfast. He had no idea that rhubarb leaves were poisonous. We went into the village on our usual weekly shopping trip and as we arrived home I rushed straight round to the back garden to see Snowball and Snowflake. Although I was only young, as soon as I saw the rabbits lying on the bottom of the hutch I knew instinctively that they were dead. I ran screaming into the kitchen calling out to my parents to come because the rabbits were dead. My mum assured me they would just be sun bathing, but followed me out into the garden and then realised that I was right. Dad went next door to see John's dad who was a keen gardener and when he told him he had given the rabbits rhubarb leaves that morning was gutted to discover that they were extremely poisonous. I cried my heart out and didn't forgive my dad for several weeks.

I'm not sure if it had anything to do with the deaths of Chirpy, Snowball and Snowflake, but I stopped asking for other pets after that. Perhaps I had a realisation that it was quite a responsibility to take care of a living creature. From then on we stuck with dogs with the exception of my pond containing newts, frogs and fish and also my collection of caterpillars which I gathered from cabbage leaves during the summer. Butch died when I was twelve after having an operation to clear a blockage in his intestines. He came home after the operation, but a week later was still very poorly and we took him back to the vets. I sat on the back seat of the car with Butch lying on a blanket next to me. As we pulled up at the vets Butch suddenly sat up, licked my face and wagged his tail. I was so thrilled and told dad he was better. Dad picked him up out of the car and Butch then died in his arms. He had summoned his last ounce of strength to sit up and say goodbye to me.

We were all so sad at losing Butch. Mum, Jayne, Brett and I were crying all day and dad didn't know what to do to comfort us. He suddenly grabbed the local paper and scoured the small ads and found an eleventh month old golden Labrador for sale. It was probably way too soon to think about getting another dog, but dad decided it was the only thing to cheer us all up. Jayne and I went with dad to see the dog and an hour or so later we brought Jason King's Ransom home with us, along with his huge bed, lead and supply of food. Jason was very handsome and turned out to be a wonderful loyal and energetic companion for us all.

I met Len when I was seventeen and at college. I still had Jason then and Len was also an animal lover and owned a cross breed called Trigger. We used to take them out together in the sand dunes and on the beach on the Norfolk coast near where we lived. I had been going out with Len for about six months and we were walking through King's Lynn one Saturday and passed a pet shop. There were various hutches outside the shop containing all sorts of animals and I noticed one with tortoises in. I stopped to look and said how much I had always wanted a tortoise so Len said he would buy me one. I was stunned by this because all my life I had been told I couldn't have whatever animal I asked for. I couldn't believe it and asked where I would be able to keep a tortoise. Len said he would build a pen and house at his home. Len's parents had a large garden with plenty of space and as they backed onto a wood there would be plenty of materials to build it out of. I was so excited after choosing my tortoise and Len built an enclosure and house for her as soon as we got back. We then decided that she would be lonely on her own so went back into town and bought a second one. We called them Bonnie and Clyde. I didn't realise it at the time but they were actually different species and so not actually suitable to keep together but in those days very little was known about tortoise husbandry and all I had to go on was the Blue Peter guide book!

It never crossed my mind at the time how cruel it was to catch wild tortoises and import them into Britain. I only discovered fairly recently that between 500,000 and one million were imported into Britain each year before a ban in the 1980s and only one or two per cent survived their first winter in hibernation. It is no wonder that they came near to extinction and are still endangered.

Bonnie and Clyde managed to survive with us for three years. Bonnie had a particularly sweet character and they moved with us to our first house near Cambridge when we got married. Our garden was a rectangle, completely enclosed and so Bonnie and Clyde could wander around freely eating whatever they fancied from the garden. We kept their little house on the terrace outside the back door and when they were ready for bed they would find their way to the path, which ran down the middle of the back garden, and walk along it until they reached the terrace and then turn towards their house and take themselves to bed. Visitors found this very amusing and were amazed to find that tortoises would do this.

Unfortunately, we had a very severe winter with heavy snow and freezing temperatures and when I got their hibernation box out of the garage was very sad to find they had not survived. We bought another tortoise later that year who turned out to be an expert escapologist. He managed to get into the vegetable garden frequently but when we moved to Burwell with a much larger garden he started to find gaps in the fences and escaped on several occasions. On the last such occasion we didn't find him again and then the import of tortoises was banned and so I felt very sad to think I would never have another one.

During the summer of 2012, I was browsing around my local garden centre for some plants when I noticed an ornamental tortoise. It was very realistic and large enough to sit on and I thought it would be a lovely addition to our garden. When I checked the price it was in the region of £160 so I decided to ask Len to buy it for me for Christmas. I dropped a few hints which seemed to fall on deaf ears and I was getting concerned it would be sold by the time he went to the garden centre so had to spell it out for him. He called in the following day and was astounded to see the price, which I had failed to mention. He decided to search the internet for a cheaper version although all he could find were baby live tortoises for sale. When he told me this I was really surprised as I didn't think it was possible to buy tortoises but he said they have to be captive bread and there were lots for sale. He went back to the garden centre and bought me the ornamental tortoise for Christmas and it did look lovely in the garden. We went on holiday shortly afterwards and wherever I went I kept seeing signs with pictures of tortoises on. I kept thinking about the idea of having another pet tortoise and felt I was getting signs from the angels that it was something I should consider.

After returning from holiday I started to search on the internet as well. I decided that rather than having a baby tortoise it would be better to get an adult one that was already used to hibernating and living in the garden during the summer. I asked the angels to help me find the right tortoise and Archangel Michael said there was a tortoise coming to me that was a very wise soul. He said it was the soul of Bonnie my first tortoise and I would be able to communicate with it. Archangel Michael told me it was male and about eight years old. Many of the tortoises for sale were many miles away from Cambridge and I didn't want to travel too far but Michael said it was very close to my home.

A couple of days later I found an eight year old male marginated tortoise for sale about four miles away. Intuitively I felt he was the right one and my dowsing confirmed this so we went to see him and he came home with us the same day. I named him Gilbert and he soon settled in with the family. The dogs were wary at first but soon accepted him. He loves the garden in the summer and has a table to live inside during Spring and Autumn until he hibernates. There is so much more information available now on the internet so it is much easier to keep tortoises happy and well. He has a small beer fridge to hibernate in. This way the temperature can be controlled and kept between five and eight degrees, which is ideal, although most people laugh when we say the tortoise is hibernating in the fridge.

During Gilbert's first hibernation with us I was able to tune in to him and communicate. Gilbert has told me that he has had many incarnations as tortoises and that is his favoured species. He was once a dinosaur though amongst other beings.

This year we decided to find a mate for Gilbert and purchased what we thought was a six year old marginated female, but within a few weeks discovered 'she' was actually a 'he'. Unfortunately, they try to bite each other so have to be kept separately.

In the intervening years between our marriage and now we have had many other pets. As the boys were growing up they would plead for pets and I generally gave in very quickly, probably because my desire for pets was never satisfied when I was young. So over the years our family have been joined by guinea pigs, gerbils, leopard geckos, ferrets, cats, a budgie and dogs.

Christian and Jason both begged us for a dog for several years. Initially we didn't feel ready to commit to having a dog but when Jason was seven years old I developed diabetes and was controlling my blood sugars by diet alone. I found that if I went for a long walk after lunch my blood sugars were much lower. I started to consider getting a dog so that I would have a reason to walk at least a couple of times a day. We decided to go to the Wood Green animal shelter near Royston to see if they had any puppies or suitable young dogs. It was towards the end of January and the shelter had been closed to the public since just before Christmas so there were plenty of dogs to choose from. Although there were no puppies at the time they invited us to have a look round. In one of the enclosures we could see about a dozen large dogs and as we went through a gate into the outer area one dog turned around and seemed to look both Len and I in the eyes. We both said simultaneously, "that's a nice dog". Len went into the enclosure on his own and this dog came up to him immediately and seemed to tell all the other dogs to keep away. We went back to the office to ask about this particular dog and were told she was an eight month old female. She had been speyed whilst there, was good with cats and children and had been at the centre for four weeks due to destructive behaviour. She was light brown in colour with a blue muzzle and ears and had a darker ridge along her back. It was thought she was a Rhodesian Ridgeback/Weimaraner cross. They assured us she had only been destructive because she was left alone all day and should grow out of it quickly, especially as I was at home all day.

Her name was Suzy and the staff brought her out to meet us all and we took her for a walk. After we satisfactorily answered the shelter's questions we were allowed to take her home that day. The boys didn't like the name Suzy and we thought it might be good to give her a new name with this new chapter in her life and so decided to rename her Shandy. She responded to her new name immediately and was extremely well behaved for about a fortnight. Once she realised she was staying she did chew up a few toys and the odd shoe, but settled very well and became a wonderful family pet. Shandy was extremely sensitive and used to stare at the blank walls in our home and it often looked as though she was following some invisible being around the room. This was before I realised we were living in a house full of ghosts! It was not until she passed over that I found out she was a High Level Being of Light who had come into a dog's body in order to assist me with animal communication. I think Earth's energies were very difficult for her at times. I realised then as well that she was meant to be our dog and that is why she knew we had come for her that day at Wood Green before we knew it ourselves.

Shandy was always quite nervous with strangers, especially men. She was a wonderful guard dog and very protective of her 'pack'. Although she was eight months old when we brought her home she had never been walked on a lead at her previous home or socialised with other dogs. We embarked on our three walks a day regime immediately and unfortunately that was too much walking too quickly for her still growing limbs and she developed an inflamed shoulder after about three months. She could run like a grey hound and no other dogs could catch up with her, which she seemed to love, but with her sore shoulder she had to stay on the lead and have short walks for several weeks. I was walking her on the lead one afternoon during this time early in the summer. I had turned down a farm track off the road where cars rarely drove. I heard a car drive past the entrance to the track then stop and reverse and turn into the track. I thought this strange, as if the driver had seen me with Shandy and decided to drive up to us. I felt a bit uneasy. I stood to the edge to allow the car to pass but the driver slowed down and unwound his window. He admired Shandy and said I should let her off the lead to have a run. I told him she was restricted to lead walking due to a shoulder injury, but he became persistent and said several times to release her from the lead. He eventually drove on but then turned round and came back towards us. Again he slowed down and told me to let her have a run off the lead. He then reached his arm out of the window towards Shandy. She growled fiercely, bared her teeth and the fur stood up along her back. She really looked like she was about to bite him. He obviously thought so as well as he quickly withdrew his arm, shut the window and drove off. I felt very relieved when he went and extremely grateful for Shandy's protective instincts. She may just have been protecting herself of course, but being on the lead I was included in that protection.

I think Shandy must have been so relieved when we finally got the ghosts cleared from our home. I certainly noticed that she was more relaxed and stopped looking at invisible beings moving through the house. After I had embarked on my clearing work she would alert me to someone coming into the house with an attachment. Even if she knew the person, if they had a soul or entity attached Shandy would start growling and I soon understood what she was telling me. Once Christian came back home from London and Len had picked him up at the station. As he walked into the house, Shandy immediately started growling with her fur standing up on her back. Christian couldn't understand what she was doing, but I realised immediately and told him he needed clearing. I was able to clear the entity before it split and jumped to me thankfully. Shandy then greeted him in her normal exuberant fashion.

One December afternoon I was delivering Christmas cards to friends in the village. One of my friends lived quite a way out of the village and in the past I had always delivered her card by car. However, it was a bright, crisp day with snow on the ground and I felt like a long walk. I walked with Shandy along the road out of the village. We had often walked along the first stretch of the road, but as we started to cover new ground Shandy became very agitated and anxious. She started to try and turn around. I got cross with her and pulled her on. We had to pass through an area of farmland before we got to the group of houses and Shandy got really frightened. I was almost at our destination so wanted to deliver the card even though I was starting to wander if I should be listening to Shandy. I managed to pull her along and pop the card into my friend's letter box and then we turned to go back. Shandy was racing along with me only just managing to hang on to the end of the lead. I was starting to feel shaky and I had a sudden pain in my head. I realised something had attached to both of us and began to regret walking there. As soon as I got back I cleared us both and it was quite a dark entity. I then managed to clear the area of land where the entity had been, so on one level it was good that it had been brought to my attention, but I decided to take more notice of Shandy in the future.

I went on my first animal communication workshop when Shandy was about thirteen years old and several months later, even though I was still practising, she was able to tell me that her time had come. Her early shoulder injury developed into arthritis when she was about twelve years old. I treated her with herbs and supplements for about eighteen months, but then she was experiencing too much pain and went onto pain killers. I knew they would destroy her liver in time but they did give her some good quality of life before then. She had been on the pain killers about eight months when she suddenly stopped eating. After refusing food for two days I dowsed her digestive organs and found them very low. Even though I did healing to boost them up, they dropped back again the following day. I talked to her and she said it was the beginning of the end. She told me she would be with us for about three more weeks and then it was time for her to go.

Despite my work and understanding of a soul's journey, it was still extremely upsetting when Shandy walked up to me one evening about three weeks later and I could see in her eyes that she was ready to go. I called the vet the next morning and arranged for them to come in the afternoon to put her down. Her legs were extremely weak but during the morning she asked to go out in the garden and found the strength to wander around saying goodbye to all her favourite places. She then settled into her bed but kept looking over her shoulder out of the back door, as if she had heard someone come through the back gate. I sat by her side savouring her last few hours with us. Strangely, just before the vet was due, I suggested to Len that he go outside and wait for them and bring them through the back way because if they rang the doorbell at the front it would cause Tia to bark and I didn't want to unsettle Shandy. Len went outside to wait for them and it then dawned on me that Shandy knew all along they would be coming in the back way.

As anyone will know who has lost a pet, their passing leaves an emptiness that cannot be filled for a while. We all have to grieve a pet's passing just as we do with a friend or family member. Shandy soon revealed herself to me as a highly evolved spiritual being whose role was to serve me with animal communication assistance. She also said that she had loved being part of our family so much that part of her soul essence would be returning in another dog. She showed me a golden cocker spaniel as her choice of incarnation and sure enough she came back to us a few months later as Honey.

Shandy died in November 2009. We had booked to go on a cruise in early January 2010 and had decided to look for a cocker spaniel puppy after we got back. It was my birthday during the cruise and Len had treated me to a massage and facial for a present. I was lying on the massage couch relaxing to soothing music when I felt a sudden sensation at the core of my being. It was like my soul had been touched. The message that Shandy's soul, or at least part of it, was back on Earth came quickly into my head. I felt quite excited and was looking forward to coming home so that I could find her. Archangel Michael confirmed that my puppy had been born and he would let me know when to look for her. The message came one day in late January and I scoured the classified ads in the local paper searching for cocker spaniel puppies. I felt despair when I couldn't find any and then Michael said to look on the internet. He said there would be signs to show me that I had found the right puppy. I searched for golden cocker spaniel puppies and I think it found over 300 matches. However, on the first page, I noticed a litter of six girls that had been born on my birthday and were at a village where I used to live in Norfolk. These were definitely the signs and my dowsing confirmed it. I rang the breeder and arranged to go and see the pups at the weekend.

When Len and I went into the breeder's kitchen we saw six identical tiny golden pups, eyes just open and crawling on their tummies in a tight huddle. I immediately started wandering how I would know which to choose when one of the pups left the group and nuzzled up to my foot. I picked her up and stroked her, still not sure if she was the right one. I placed her back with her sisters but she turned back and made her way to my feet again. The breeder remarked that she had obviously chosen me and that seemed enough of a sign so we decided on her. Four weeks later we collected Honey and brought her home. It felt wonderful to have two dogs once again.

I cannot finish my chapter on animals without another mention of Tia. She has the most wonderful temperament of any dog I have ever known. Jenny, a good friend of mine had a collie cross bitch who suffered with phantom pregnancies and she decided it would be best for her to have a litter before she was speyed. Whilst she was in season a pedigree black Labrador who lived just round the corner managed to escape from his garden and the pair ran off together in the fields. Several weeks later a litter of twelve little black pups were born. One died after a couple of days and I called in to see the eleven remaining pups when they were about two weeks old. Jenny had to find eleven good homes for them and tried to persuade me several times to have one of the pups. I visited Tia and her siblings about three times in the following few weeks by which time I was completely besotted.

About ten days after bringing Tia home Shandy bit her on the nose one morning. Tia was used to snuggling up with her siblings in one large bed and couldn't understand why Shandy wanted her bed to herself. Each morning she tried to nuzzle her way in until Shandy decided to put Tia in her place. I was distraught to find blood pouring from Tia's nose and we called the emergency vet as it was about 6.00 am. The vet suggested we bring her to the surgery when it opened at 9.00 am. I was running a stall that day at a healing fair so had to leave her with Len. He called me to say Tia had been given an injection and he was to keep her quiet and watch her which he did. When I got back home just after 5:00 pm Tia hadn't moved all day and was still quiet in bed. Len thought we should call the vet out but I suggested I do some healing first. I used my SRT direct healing and colours chart and downloaded all that my Higher Self directed me to. I came down stairs ten minutes later and Tia jumped up out of bed and wanted to go into the garden. She was running around like a nine week old puppy once again as if nothing was wrong. Len was amazed how quickly the healing had worked.

Tia has been very healthy all her life, but another time my healing was needed was after she was speyed. She lay in her bed looking so down and depressed even though it was several days since the operation. Caroline Izzard happened to call me for a chat and I mentioned how Tia was. Caroline 'saw' immediately that there was a weakness in Tia's aura where the anaesthetic had been administered and she recommended I heal that part of her aura and then neutralise the anaesthetic still in her body. I did what Caroline recommended and later that day Tia was her lively self once again.

Tia looks just like a pedigree black labrador but on closer examination she has a longer nose and has always had some white hairs on her back legs and tummy. She is so gentle and has never snapped or growled in all her nine years even when she was being attacked once by a border collie. She was also the most tolerant dog imaginable when we brought Honey home. She let Honey crawl all over her, nibble her ears and grab at her jowls and has never once told her off. The pair of them are very close and Honey adores her but then she does have part of Shandy's soul.

"God Bless Animals, for
They are Essential to the Balance of Nature"
Reprinted with permission from *Daily Word*® **UK**

CHAPTER

Imprints

It was actually Shandy who first taught me about imprints. Although I dowsed about them and often found them on land and houses, especially when there had been battles or a lot of suffering in the past, Shandy showed me their existence.

Whenever we went away on holiday Shandy went to stay with Len's parents, who lived in Norfolk near the woods at Sandringham. Shandy was far too nervous to stay in kennels but loved spending time with them. Len's parents had always had dogs and they had a Yorkshire Terrier called Buttons, just a few months older than Shandy, so they were wonderful playmates for each other.

Before Buttons time they had owned a couple of German Shepherds and Len's dad had built a run and kennel in the garden. Unfortunately, one of the German Shepherds, Jet, developed a brain tumour and had obviously experienced pain and discomfort before they were aware how ill he was. He appeared to be mentally unwell and it was very sad when he had to be put down. They didn't get another dog for a while afterwards and so the run and kennel were dismantled and a summer house was built on the concrete base. Being a wonderful sun trap, Len's parents often sat out there with afternoon tea and Buttons would happily join them. After one of our holidays we went to collect Shandy and they mentioned that Shandy loved to sit on the lawn but would never step foot inside the summer house. Even if they coaxed her with a biscuit she would reach forward to take the treat, making sure her feet didn't cross the threshold. They were puzzled by this although immediately it came into my mind that Jet would have left an imprint when it was his run. Although I had healed their home previously I hadn't looked for imprints in the garden. I told them I would do some work on clearing it which I did later that evening.

The following summer Shandy went to stay again when we went on holiday. When we collected her Len's parents told me how she happily came into the summer house now when they sat out there. I reminded them about the imprint I had cleared, which we had all forgotten about, and Shandy's behaviour showed me how real it was and confirmed that it was now gone.

I had another lesson about imprints a few months after Shandy had passed. Before we got Honey we decided to move Tia's bed to the space Shandy had slept in as the puppy crate would only fit where Tia had been sleeping. Tia was quite happy in her new space and Honey slept in the crate when we got her. After about five months I came downstairs one morning and Tia came up to me but with a limp. Her left shoulder looked sore and she reminded me of Shandy with her left arthritic shoulder. Tia was only five years old and had not had any problems with her joints at all. I realised in a flash that Shandy had left an imprint of 'painful left shoulder' where she slept. I dowsed that this was correct and cleared the imprint. I gave healing to Tia and the next morning she was fine again.

A couple of weeks later I was going upstairs and my knees were feeling particularly painful. Since moving into our cottage in 2000 my knees had got steadily worse and I regularly put healing into the joints. This helped for a few weeks and then needed to be repeated. I often thought that I would have to move to a bungalow eventually as my knees seemed to be deteriorating. As I pulled myself up the stairs with the help of the banister it struck me that this might also be an imprint. The elderly couple who we bought the cottage from were moving to a bungalow because of the wife's painful knees!

I dowsed about this and it was confirmed. There were imprints in the cottage of painful knees and I had picked these imprints up just like Tia picked up an imprint left by Shandy. I cleared the imprints and then checked every room in the house to make sure all imprints were cleared. My knees have been so much better since it is amazing. This showed me how important it is to clear imprints from all houses because if people or animals have ever lived on the land then they will almost certainly have left some imprints behind. After healing houses for people I often get comments like, "my back ache is so much better", or "the problem I had with my foot has completely gone", and I realise now that these were all imprints and not actually the person's problem.

"I Am Healed and Renewed"
Reprinted with permission from *Daily Word®* UK

Mobile Masts And Wi Fi Energies

I had been healing houses successfully for a number of years and wasn't expecting the angels to bring me any new lessons, but they did just that early in 2008. Jason and his girlfriend had been looking into buying a flat and as he was only nineteen years old, both Len and I felt he was too young to tie himself down. Luckily, they had the offer to house sit a flat in Cambridge for six months so we thought it would be a good trial run for them to see how they managed paying rent and utility bills. I healed the flat for them and we helped them decorate the lounge and bedroom and it felt fine being there for a few hours. We helped them move in during the first week of January and the energies seemed to be good. We left them to get sorted out and Jason came back the following afternoon to collect some personal items. When I asked how his first night had been he said neither of them had slept a wink. I thought this was just because it was about getting settled into a new place and didn't think any more about it. Towards the end of the week they came to us for dinner and I was amazed to hear that still neither of them had slept at all. A little voice in my head said that there was something new to learn, but I dismissed this right away because I didn't want Jason to be used as a 'guinea pig'. My conscious mind decided that there had to be something I had missed and thought this was most likely to be a 'sink place'. A sink place is a natural drain for negative energy in the Earth and they don't cause a problem unless they are sited under somebody's bed or chair. When I find them in such a position I ask the angels to re-route them to a more suitable location. I 'found' a sink place under their bed and asked the angels to move it for me. It is amazing how the conscious mind can control the pendulum when you let it take over.

This made no difference to their sleeping, so I then decided that I must have missed a broken ley line. Again, I managed to find one and heal it. Still they were both exhausted with complete lack of sleep and came back to stay with us to get a good night's rest. I then decided to repeat the whole healing process in case something else had been missed. I felt sure this would do the trick, but a couple of weeks later Jason rang to say that if they didn't get any sleep soon, they would leave the flat and move back with us. With the thought of moving all their stuff back again and on hearing that inner voice telling me once again that I had to learn something new, I surrendered to the Universe and said, "Ok, please tell me what at Jason's flat is stopping them sleeping". Immediately I saw a picture in my mind of the tower at the hospital in Cambridge covered in mobile masts. This was only about half a mile from the flat as the crow flies. Straight away I thought it must be the emissions from all the mobile masts and was just about to go upstairs and dowse when the 'phone rang. I answered to find a new customer saying that her sleep was badly affected by mobile mast emissions and things had got a lot worse just after Christmas when the 3G upgrade came in. The Universe was sending me immediate confirmation. I told the lady that I could dowse and heal the negative energies in the house but I was still working on how to shield people from mobile mast emissions. I began working with the angels to find out what I needed to do. Over the following few weeks I had several more enquiries, all from people who had started to experience sleep problems at the start of the year. Most people reported that their brains felt wired.

It took me about three weeks to get the process right and my confirmation that it had worked was when Jason and his girlfriend had finally started to sleep in the flat. About a month later Jason rang to say that he was moving back home as he had decided he was too young to settle down! It was as if the Universe guided him to move in with his girlfriend just so I could learn about protecting homes from mobile masts.

A couple of months later an existing client called to say her sleep had suddenly deteriorated again even though I had shielded her from mobile masts. She knew that her neighbour had installed Wi Fi and was certain it was affecting her brain at night. I managed to work out a technique to shield from these energies fairly quickly and my client's extreme sensitivity confirmed that the process was right. I then started to follow my earth healing with shielding from these types of energies for all the properties I tackled.

Jason found that once he had moved back home his sleep was never as deep and restful as it had been before he lived temporarily in the flat. My dowsing investigations came up with the fact that his melatonin levels were much lower than they should be and also his pineal gland function was considerably lower. I worked on improving his pineal gland over a number of healing sessions and he also took melatonin for a few months. His sleep eventually improved although he says it is still not as good as it used to be. My theory is that when the brain is suddenly bombarded with strong levels of mobile mast emissions it affects the pineal gland and the electrical impulses that normally release melatonin. With healing and shielding it is possible to keep people protected from these energies, but I do feel very concerned about the percentage of the population that are having their brains overloaded on a nightly basis, especially the young whose brains are still developing.

"For Every Problem, There is A Spiritual Solution"

CHAPTER

Dark Entities

I wasn't sure whether to include any more about dark entities in this book but the angels have told me to do so. I am often asked after clearing a house or a person to explain what exactly a dark entity is. From my experiences I have discovered that it may or may not be of human origin. It no longer has a body so is 'discarnate', whereas we are 'incarnate' when we are alive in a body. All dark entities are frightened of the Light and so they will not pass to the Light with ease. Before I did my SRT work the angels taught me some clearing procedures for dark entities and told me that they need to go to a place of the Light but not in the Light, so they can unlearn their dark ways. I developed clearances for several types of dark entity but found the darkest ones, the demonics, the most difficult to clear. I scoured spiritual books for information about dark entities, but found that most authors steered well away from the subject. I did find out some useful information in a book by Louise Ireland-Frey called Freeing the Captives. This led me to work with a specialist guide who communicated with the demonic entity for me and although it sometimes worked it was not always successful. Soon after this I went on the SRT course and found out that demonics usually lie and it is unwise to try and clear them with communication. Although many people think of these entities as being pure evil, I have found that they are just so enmeshed in darkness that they have forgotten there is still Light at the core of their being. They are fear based beings and feed off people's fear. They enjoy causing accidents and arguments and creating general disharmony. After they have been cleared I see them as being held in a type of 'Borstal' where they can be reformed until they are ready to forgive themselves and move back to the Light and be fully reintegrated in the Light. Once they have been cleared they cannot come back to Earth, but only move on to the Light when they are ready.

If people experience a lot of problems with dark entities then it is usually either because their house is built on land where unpleasant things have happened, or they have past life connections with the dark side which need to be cleared. We cannot know the Light unless we have experienced the Dark and so many Lightworkers today will have had lives working for the dark side and these will need to be cleared so they can be free to move forwards working for the Light. We often still have contracts in place from a time when we worked with a dark being and these need to be broken in order for us to work fully in the Light. I had many lives to clear where I worked with the dark and also several contracts with dark masters but once they were all cleared and along with it all fear energies within my sub conscious, I was able to stay clear and protected.

"The Light of God Shines Bright in Me"
Reprinted with permission from *Daily Word*® **UK**

CHAPTER

Amber's Story

I have included some case histories throughout the book, but Amber's story merits a chapter by itself.

Amber's mother Wendy rang me one morning having been given my name by a Bowen therapist near to where she lived. She had taken Amber to see the therapist because her daughter had suffered from severe headaches for several years. Her headaches started quite suddenly when Amber was eight years old and by the time she was eleven years old she was diagnosed as having migraines. The headaches were incredibly debilitating and prevented her sleeping so she was constantly tired and could only attend school for afternoon sessions. The headaches grew worse and by the time she was fourteen years old she was diagnosed with cluster headaches. The hospital said that it was very unusual for a child to get cluster headaches. Amber had undergone numerous tests in hospital over the years but no cause for them could be found. After the diagnosis of cluster headaches one of the nurses asked Wendy if she had tried any alternative treatments for

Amber. Wendy hadn't known what to try and had thought it better to remain with orthodox treatment but the nurse suggested that she contact a Bowen therapist who had great success in treating people with headaches. This therapist lived many miles away from me but had attended one of my workshops in the past and was well aware of the effects of spirit attachment.

Wendy took Amber along for her first session and in the initial consultation Amber told the therapist that there was a ghost girl at home who she thought may be causing her problems. This was the first time Amber had mentioned such a thing and Wendy was astonished to hear about the ghost. Amber then blurted out what had happened many years earlier.

Amber told her mum that she knew exactly the day the ghost first came into her life. She was eight years old at the time and they were taking her older brother for a piano lesson and had dropped him off at the teacher's house. Wendy then took Amber to a park nearby to play on the swings. As Amber approached the swings a young girl of similar age emerged from the hedge. Amber knew she was a ghost. The ghost had long, straight black hair with a fringe and was wearing a dirty white smock over a dress. She had bare legs and feet and Amber felt sorry for her not having any shoes or boots of any kind. She had dark staring eyes and in fact looked quite menacing. The most frightening thing about her was that she was holding a large knife, blade pointing upwards.

Amber felt very uneasy so went to play on the slide and roundabout but the ghost followed her around wherever she went. When Wendy and Amber got back into the car to go and collect her brother, the ghost got into the car with them. She travelled back home with them and followed Amber into her house. The ghost then shadowed Amber wherever she went. She would wake Amber up at night and frighten her. She would follow her to school, watch her in the shower and bath and in fact never leave her in peace.

In hindsight, Wendy told me that Amber's problems began when she was eight years old. She started to be frightened of going to bed on her own and began having nightmares and night terrors. The headaches began at this time as well.

Unfortunately, for whatever reason, Amber kept this knowledge about the ghost to herself and suffered tremendously over many years of her childhood.

When she finally spilled out her story in the therapist's room, Wendy was amazed at what had been happening. She told me later on the phone that Amber experienced episodes of uncontrollable behaviour where in the past she had torn curtains down, smashed ornaments and used terrible language that she wouldn't normally have known.

The therapist told Amber that she knew someone who would be able to help take the ghost away to where it needed to go. Wendy took down my phone number and called me as soon as she was back at home. As she recounted the story to me I could see the ghost in my mind's eye and got the message that she had murdered someone when she was alive, even though only a young child herself. I suggested to Wendy that I do the clearing about 10:00 pm that night and told her it should only take about fifteen minutes. She explained to Amber about the clearing and Amber was worried that the ghost was going to be annoyed. This obviously created a lot of fear within Amber about the process.

As arranged, I began the clearing later that evening. I had wondered if the ghost was a dark entity but found out it was only an earthbound soul. However, as I began the clearing I discovered that the ghost had a demonic entity attached to her and I then realised that this demonic would have caused her to commit the murder and remain earthbound.

As my pendulum swung I could see the ghost girl stabbing Amber in the top of her head. I knew this would be causing terrible pain for Amber and realised that all her headaches were the result of this psychic attack. My pendulum slowed down and I was able to confirm that the ghost had gone. I repaired holes and tears in Amber's aura and cleansed her through and gave her healing. This ghost had been attached to Amber but it was interesting for me to learn that Amber could see the ghost in front of her, behind her or around the room somewhere, not just shadowing her which is what I always imagined an attached spirit would do. It had not taken much longer for me to clear than usual and I assumed all would be calm and better for Amber that night.

I rang Wendy in the morning to tell her what I had done and find out what their experience had been. Wendy said that Amber had been very frightened and worried about the ghost's reaction and sure enough as the clearing started Amber felt the ghost stabbing her in the head. She was crying out in extreme pain and this went on until about 3 am. I realised that even though I had finished at my end, Amber's fear was preventing the ghost from being released easily and so the angels were having a hard time in removing her. Eventually things settled and Amber was able to go to bed.

Wendy called me the following day to say they had all had a good night and that Amber had woken up in the night and could see herself surrounded by a ring of friends, maybe angels or fairies. The ghost then appeared in her bedroom but this time she looked clean, the knife was no longer in her hands, she was smiling and wearing brand new shiny boots! Amber was so pleased that she had some footwear at last. The ghost smiled at Amber again and said 'thank you' and then disappeared. Amber told Wendy that she knew now that the ghost had only come to her for help and she was now at peace and she felt she had complete closure on the whole episode. Her headaches have not returned since and she is now aware that if she ever gets followed by a ghost again she must get help immediately.

"I Am Fearless, Strong and Free"
Reprinted with permission from *Daily Word*® **UK**

CHAPTER

My Divine Life Mission

My journey has been difficult at times, but has brought me to fulfil my Divine life mission; that is being an energy healer. Along the way I have become qualified in a number of healing modalities, but still the bulk of my work is doing what the Angels taught me – healing sick houses. I do this work all over the world and have a constant stream of new clients and properties waiting to be touched by the Angels.

Our precious planet has been plundered and abused over the years. The Earth is like one huge body that has absorbed every painful experience created and received by man and animals over the centuries. All the wars and fighting have left their mark. The planet is saturated with pain and negativity, layer upon layer through history. Some places are literally toxic as one negative action attracts another, leaving dark energies and entities to cause disharmony for the people who unknowingly settle in such places. I say unknowingly even though on a soul level many people are drawn to such places as a means of awakening, like me, or to clear karma. Often a person will have lived in the area in a past life and contributed to the cause of some of the negative energies and once they have passed over into the Light they will make a contract to return and live in the place to suffer, clearing their karma in the process, until they become aware of what is needed. Many of my clients have been in a situation where they are unable to sell and move away from their house until they arrange for it to be cleared and healed. Once you have fulfilled your contract and brought about the release of stuck souls and healing to the land, your house attracts the right buyer and you are free to move on.

I take great pleasure in my work. It is lovely to work with Angels and so rewarding to transform the energies from detrimental to beneficial, hearing wonderful feedback from my clients about how their lives start to change for the better almost immediately.

Once one of my clients asked me to explain in more detail how I had done the earth healing and I mentioned that a six pointed star, filled with Divine Light, was placed under each property that I worked on. She remarked "you're lighting up the planet like stars in the night sky" which I thought was a beautiful image. Little by little these stars are spreading the Light helping to heal the whole of our beautiful Mother Earth.

"I Am Wings of Freedom"

ABOUT THE AUTHOR

Debbie Rye began her working life as a secretary in Cambridge. She left work in 1984 to have her first child and was a full time mother for several years.

In her search for the answers to a number of health issues, she learned about detrimental energies and began working with angels to heal them. She has developed techniques to clear and heal buildings around the world.

This is Debbie's first book. She currently lives in Cambridgeshire, England with her husband, Len, doing her energy healing work.

RESOURCES

Debbie Rye
Earth Energy Healing, Entity Clearance
www.alternativeways.co.uk

Anne Jones
Author, Spiritual Teacher, Healer www.annejones.org

Pamilla Cobb
Author www.surfingrainbows.com

Daily Word
A Unity Publication www.unityuk.org
Unity is a world-wide spiritual movement not allied to any church, sect
or denomination

Jayne Franz
Channelled Angel Art
www.alternativeways.co.uk\angelart